WHITE HOUSE BRIDES

WHITE

HOUSE BRIDES

By Marie Smith and Louise Durbin

Washington Post Staff Writers

published by

ACROPOLIS BOOKS

A DIVISION OF COLORTONE PRESS

COLORTONE BUILDING—2400 17TH ST., N. W.
WASHINGTON, D. C. 20009

AMERICANA
by ACROPOLIS

   ACROPOLIS BOOKS
   Colortone Building, 2400 17th St., N. W.
   Washington, D. C. 20009

Printed in the United States of America by
Colortone Creative Printing, Washington, D. C. 20009

Type set in Caledonia with
Century Schoolbook Bold chapter headings.

Library of Congress Catalog Number 66-29548

TO OUR MOTHERS

Dessie Marr Smith
Elsie Wood Durbin

This American Ballad Bowl of Steuben Glass designed by George Thompson and the design engraved by Sidney Waugh was presented by the House of Representatives to the 1966 White House Bride Luci Johnson Nugent. Engraved around the bowl are four scenes portraying the pioneering history and settlement of the United States: Exploration, Colonization, Independence and Expansion.

Acknowledgments

The authors are particularly indebted to the following individuals and institutions for material, advice and encouragement in the preparation of this book:

Marie Sauer, women's editor of *The Washington Post*, who let us do a newspaper series on White House Brides, from which this book evolved.

The White House.

Massachusetts Historical Society, Boston, Mass.—quotations from the unpublished Adams Papers are from the microfilm edition, by permission of the Massachusetts Historical Society.

The Belknap Press of Harvard University Press, Cambridge, Mass., for permission to reprint quotations from *The Diary of Charles Francis Adams*, Aida and David Donald, editors, copyright 1964 *Massachusetts Historical Society.*

Yale University Library, University of Alabama Library, Mrs. Waldo Johnston, Lynn Johnston, John Augustine Washington, Dr. John Augustine Washington, Mrs. Augustine Jacqueline Todd, Mr. and Mrs. Laurence Gouverneur Hoes.

The James Monroe Memorial Library and Law Office, Fredericksburg, Virginia, *Mrs. Ralph H. Dillon, Mrs. Trezvant Yeatman, Hamilton Place*, Columbia, Tennessee, *Mrs. John De Saussure, Mrs. Reginald Knapp, Mrs. Carl G. Mortenson, George Harrison Sanford King, John I. Coddington, Princess Julia Cantacuzene, General Ulysses S. Grant III, Mrs. Nicholas Longworth, Mrs. Isaac Stuart McElroy, Jr., Mrs. James Halsted, Mrs. Allin Baxter.*

Margaret Brown Klapthor, associate curator, Division of Political History, The Smithsonian Institution, *Renata V. Shaw*, Prints and Photographs Division, Library of Congress, *L. H. Butterfield*, editor in chief, The Adams Papers, *Marc Friedlaender*, associate editor, The Adams Papers.

Watt C. Marchman, director, The Rutherford B. Hayes Library, Fremont, Ohio, *The Smithsonian Institution, Library of Congress, National Park Service, Department of the Interior, National Trust for Historic Preservation, National Archives.*

The authors and the publisher also wish to thank The Washington Post for permission to republish portions of this book which were prepared originally for The Washington Post and published therein.

Introduction

The White House at 1600 Pennsylvania Avenue in Washington, D.C., is the symbol of the nation's executive power. It is also a home for those few families whose head is the President of the United States. And as a home, it has been the setting for many romances, courtships and marriages.

Three Presidents wooed and won while living in the White House. Eight Presidential daughters were married while living in the mansion. On six of these occasions, beginning with Maria Hester Monroe in 1820, the daughters have chosen the White House itself as the scene for their wedding. One daughter, Anna Roosevelt Dall, went to her family's home in New York for the ceremony, and the most recent Presidential daughter to wed, Luci Baines Johnson, had a church wedding followed by a reception in the White House.

The White House was only 12 years old when the first wedding of record was held there. That was in 1812 when a widow named Lucy Payne Washington, sister of First Lady Dolley Madison, married a Supreme Court Justice. But that is only the beginning of the history of romance that has swirled through the corridors of the mansion. A Presidential son, nieces and friends of Presidents have been married there. Others were married elsewhere and brought their brides to visit or live in the President's House.

Some of these White House brides were gay, some gauche. Some beautiful, some painfully plain. More than one was a merry widow.

Presidential families like other families have had their problems. President Jackson had to call back the invitations to a wedding and then issue new ones when a young niece changed her mind. President Grant gave his daughter away with tears in his eyes because her choice sorely troubled him. President John Quincy Adams was host at a wedding that split his closely knit family asunder. One young man, Francis Bowes Sayre, had trouble getting into the White House grounds an hour before the wedding because the guards refused to believe he was the bridegroom.

To recreate this romantic part of the nation's history—a part that has been full of secrecy, frustration and love—the authors have dug deeply into old chronicles, diaries and albums in the Library of Congress and the National Archives and in the possession of descendants. They have interviewed some of the brides themselves, who provided lively reminiscences of that important event in their lives, their wedding. They have found photographs of every bride, even in cases where experts said photographs did not exist, to show what these women of history looked like. Many are pictured in their wedding gown.

This is their story—the White House brides—presented for the first time under one cover and in chronological order to provide a richer flavor of history and a setting of the times.

M.S.-L.D.

Washington, D.C.

CONTENTS

I

The First
White House
Wedding of Record

Lucy Payne Washington - Thomas Todd
March 29, 1812

 bride named Lucy stole the spotlight—for a day—from President James Madison and his Dolley in the first White House wedding of record. The bride was Lucy Payne Washington and her wedding took place on March 29, 1812, in the original President's mansion before it was burned by the British during the war in 1814. The bridegroom was Supreme Court Justice Thomas Todd, a widower from Frankfort, Kentucky, whose family had been Virginians.

Lucy was the widowed sister of Dolley Madison, the "Queen" of the "Palace" as the President's mansion was called. Lucy might have been doomed to wear widow's weeds the rest of her life, but sister Dolley had other ideas. So the young widow moved into the mansion with the Madisons for a prolonged visit. There she was not only a welcome member of the family circle but a delightful addition to the social life of Dolley Madison's drawing rooms, which were flavored with a stately elegance and a courtly grace. For the hallmarks of royalty were still stamped on the manners and modes of speech of the best society in the young nation's capital.

It was a far cry from the severely plain Quaker upbringing that Lucy and Dolley Payne knew when they were little girls in Virginia and later in Philadelphia.

Their father was John Payne II, the son of an English gentleman of wealth and education who immigrated to the colonies and settled on the James River in Goochland County, Virginia. John left home at an early age to manage family land holdings in North Carolina. There he took his bride, Mary Coles, whose father, William Coles, had emigrated from En-

Lucy Payne Washington, the first White House Bride of record. She was married to Supreme Court Justice Thomas Todd on March 29, 1812.

niscorthy, Ireland, and founded a plantation called Coles Hill in Virginia. John Payne won his suit for the beautiful Mary's hand against heavy competition, for the talented young Thomas Jefferson was one of Miss Mary's admirers. Her cousin, Patrick Henry, was also a handsome member of this circle of young friends.

Little Dolley was born in North Carolina—where her parents were visiting—and named for her mother's aunt, Mrs. Patrick Henry. Lucy was born in Virginia, where her father had purchased an estate in Hanover County within driving distance of Coles Hill. Four other children were born to John and Mary Payne, and they spent their early years in quiet simplicity in their Virginia country home.

The little girls were great favorites of their grandmother, who surreptitiously slipped them pretty presents of old-fashioned jewelry, which savored too much "of the vanities" to suit their parents, who were strict members of the Society of Friends. Lucy and Dolley sewed the forbidden baubles into little bags, which they tied around their necks and kept hidden beneath their plain little frocks.

Before they trotted off to the country school, their mother carefully put sunbonnets on their pretty heads, with white linen masks to screen every ray of sunshine from their complexions, and long gloves to protect the hands and arms. Concealed beneath their prim little gray dresses were the precious bags of forbidden jewels, so treasured by the little Payne sisters.

Legend has it that the greatest calamity in Dolley's childhood was the day the string of her little bag became unfastened, scattering her treasures through the woods on the way to school. Days of searching for the lost jewels proved in vain.

Their father was called a fanatic, for he was one of the first Quakers in Virginia to become opposed to slavery. He sold his plantation and gave freedom to his slaves, but several devoted servants refused to leave the Paynes and these he took with the family when they moved to Philadelphia, the Quaker city of brotherly love, in 1783.

There John Payne brought up his children and educated them at schools taught by the Quaker sect, which forbade frivolity and ornamentation of all kinds. And there, like a dutiful Quaker daughter, Dolley Payne unquestioningly obeyed her father's request that she marry a good-looking young Quaker lawyer of means, John Todd, Jr. The wedding took place on January 27, 1790, in the Friends' Meeting House on Pine Street.

John Payne died in 1791 and his widow took gentlemen boarders into her home on Third Street in Philadelphia. But it was not long until there was another wedding in the family. For Lucy had turned into a lovely young lady, and beneath her prim little Quaker cap was tucked a headful of pretty brown curls surrounding a piquant round face that was pleasing to look at.

Philadelphia was now the nation's capital and one of the young men about town was George Steptoe Washington. He was a favorite nephew of General George Washington and had inherited from his father, Colonel Samuel Washington, the Harewood plantation in Berkeley County, Virginia, near present-day Charles Town, West Virginia.

Supreme Court Justice Thomas Todd. Reproduced from an etching.

Lucy Payne won both the heart of the courtly George Steptoe Washington and her mother's consent to marry him. He was not a Quaker, so Lucy turned her back on the formidable regulations of the Friends' church and was married in St. Paul's Church on May 20, 1793, with the Rev. Dr. McGaw performing the ceremony. The marriage brought the strict criticism of the rigid Quakers down upon Lucy, and she was promptly "read out of meeting" by members of the Society of Friends.

It was probably with relief that Lucy left Philadelphia with her husband to make her home in Virginia, the land of her birth and early childhood.

Four months later Dolley was left a widow when she lost both her husband and a child in an epidemic of fever that swept Philadelphia. In the course of time, after she recovered from a serious bout of the fever, Dolley attracted eligible admirers. James Madison, a bachelor 20 years her senior, won the young widow's promise in September 1794.

It was probably recent memories of Lucy's wedding "out of meeting"—and the unpleasantness surrounding it—that prompted Dolley to drive to Lucy's and George Steptoe Washington's home in the beautiful Shenandoah Valley for her own Episcopal wedding to Mr. Madison.

There in the paneled parlor of the Harewood stone planta-tion home Dolley Payne Todd was married to James Madison.

Legend has it that one of the wedding guests was Lighthorse Harry Lee, who came galloping up just in time for the ceremony.

Lucy herself was left a widow with three small children in 1809. By that time her sister Dolley's husband was President James Madison, and Lucy came occasionally to live in the Executive Mansion in Washington. Also a frequent visitor was their younger sister, Anna, who had lived with Dolley until her marriage to Congressman Richard Cutts of the Massachusetts district that is now Maine.

Once a guest in the "blazing splendor of Mrs. Madison's drawing room," Washington Irving described Dolley's radiant sisters, Lucy Washington and Anna Cutts, as being "like the two merry wives of Windsor; but as to Jemmy Madison—ah poor Jemmy!—he is but a withered little apple-john."

During the winter months of 1812 Judge Thomas Todd, who had been appointed to the Supreme Court by President Jefferson in 1807, pursued the blooming widow Washington in a White House courtship but was refused when he proposed marriage. The rejected Judge packed his carriage and left Washington for his old Kentucky home.

Then the lady changed her mind, hastily dispatching a letter by a special messenger on horseback who caught up with the Judge at Lancaster, Pennsylvania.

When Judge Todd read the merry widow's letter of acceptance, telling him she was willing "to be a second prey," he promptly turned the carriage around and returned to the capital. Some ten days later they were married.

Dolley returned the favor Lucy had done for her some 18 years before at Harewood and gave a wedding fit for the "Queen's" sister in the President's mansion.

The Rev. Andrew T. McCormick performed the Episcopal marriage ceremony in a Sunday evening wedding. Three bridesmaids and three groomsmen attended the couple.

The bridesmaids were Phoebe Morris of Philadelphia, a Mrs. Hamilton and Mrs. Hay, probably Mrs. Alexander Hamilton and Mrs. George Hay, the elder daughter of the James Monroes. The groomsmen were Dolley's son, Payne Todd; a cousin of the Payne sisters, a Mr. Coles, probably Edward Coles, who was serving as private secretary to President Madison and was later Governor of Illinois; and a brother of the Payne sisters, probably John Payne.

The next morning the carriage took off again for Kentucky, this time with a stop en route at Harewood. When she arrived in Kentucky, Lucy was delighted with her new home and wrote glowing reports to Dolley.

When the Supreme Court sat in Washington the winter of 1813-14, one of its justices was missing. "Judge Todd . . . has remained with my dear Lucy to nurse their young daughter of whom they are very proud," Dolley related happily in a letter to Phoebe Morris. The child "is called Madisonia Dolley. The last name I am determined shall be left out when they come to me next summer," Aunt Dolley decided. Later records show the little girl's name as Dorothea Madisonia.

Little Dorothea, who was born on December 15, 1813, was married in 1839 to Charles Quinn and later divorced him. Other children born to Lucy and Thomas Todd were William Johnston Todd in 1815 and James Madison Todd in 1818.

Lucy had had four sons by her first marriage to George Steptoe Washington—a son George, who died as a baby, Samuel Walter, William Temple and George Steptoe, Jr.

Thomas Todd died in 1826. Lucy outlived him by 20 years. She died in her seventies at Harewood. The handsome old stone plantation home still stands in the Shenandoah Valley and is owned by descendants of Lucy and her first husband, George Steptoe Washington.

An English engraving of the White House as it looked when Dolley Madison gave her sister, Lucy Payne Washington, a wedding there. Supreme Court Justice Thomas Todd of Kentucky was the bridegroom.

17

II

The First
Presidential
Daughter to Wed

Maria Hester Monroe - Samuel Lawrence Gouverneur
March 9, 1820

highhanded elder sister made something of an international incident out of the first White House wedding of a President's daughter when Maria Hester Monroe and her first cousin, Samuel Lawrence Gouverneur, were married on March 9, 1820.

The social storm stirred by Eliza Hay, Maria's older sister, very nearly matched the wind-lashed rain of that March wedding day.

The Episcopal ceremony was performed by the Rev. William Hawley, rector of St. John's Church on Lafayette Square, before only "the family and friends." Not even the Cabinet was invited, and certainly not the Diplomatic Corps.

Eliza, who lived at the White House with her husband, George Hay, and child, was having a feud with the Diplomatic Corps, or at least the wives of its members. It was not the first tangle the domineering Eliza had with the Diplomatic Corps but another in a long chain of incidents over protocol.

Probably no President had as much trouble with questions of etiquette as James Monroe. His difficulties grew directly out of the views of the women in his family, particularly Eliza, about the social obligations of the President and his family.

"This senseless war of etiquette-visiting," as Secretary of State John Quincy Adams described it, was discussed in at least two Cabinet meetings. Caught in the middle of the maelstrom was Adams and his wife, Louisa Catherine, who served as intermediaries between the difficult Eliza and the Diplomatic Corps.

It started when Mrs. Monroe, who was not in good health when she moved into the White House, decided not to follow

---

Maria Hester Monroe from the James Monroe Memorial Library, Fredericksburg, Virginia.

the popular Dolley Madison's practice of paying first calls on wives of members of the Diplomatic Corps.

Mrs. Monroe not only did not pay first calls, she did not return calls either. She preferred to lead a retiring life within the White House walls and receive company there. This left the First Family's social obligations to the pretty and perverse Eliza, who acted as proxy for her ailing mother. Eliza had been splendidly educated at Madame Campan's boarding school in France while her father served as U.S. Minister there and was well-qualified to be a White House hostess had it not been for her domineering ways.

Eliza returned White House calls made on her mother, but never made the first call. Since the diplomats' wives in turn refused to call on Eliza first, a social stalemate resulted. This was the situation when Maria's wedding plans were made.

The night before the wedding the Russian Minister Poletica inquired of Mrs. Adams when the diplomats might pay their respects to the bridal couple. Eliza was incensed to learn that the Diplomatic Corps would make a distinction between her and her sister. She declared that if they did come to the White House receptions honoring the bride, their calls should not be returned. Consequently, Mrs. Adams told the diplomats they were to take no notice of the wedding.

Whether the President spoke to her about the matter is not known, but a few days later Eliza relented. On the Monday after the wedding, which took place on Thursday, she dispatched a messenger to Mrs. Adams to say that the diplomats and their wives would be allowed to attend that evening's "drawing room" (the term used for reception in those days). Still in fighting trim, she added that the bride and her husband "would condescend to return the visits but that there would be no public intercourse between them."

Thinking the message was for her husband, Mrs. Adams did nothing about speeding the new ruling on its way until he came home that night. By that time it was too late to notify the diplomats of the change. When Eliza learned they had not received the message, she decided they should not be invited a second time. So the diplomats and their wives were not given an opportunity to congratulate the bridal couple.

This engraving by W. I. Stone, published by Peter Force in Washington in 1820, shows the north front of the White House at the time of the wedding of the first presidential daughter, Maria Monroe, there.

The White House was a beautiful setting for Maria Monroe's wedding. It had been renovated not for the nuptials but because the British had left it charred after the War of 1812.

There were no traces of that 1814 fire, however, when the young couple married, surrounded by the French-gilt furniture made to specifications for the White House at President Monroe's order by Pierre-Antoine Bellangé, the finest cabinetmaker in Paris.

Some writers say the ceremony was held in the still unfurnished East Room, others that it took place in the oval drawing room where the couple stood on an Aubusson carpet dominated by the design of an enormous American eagle.

The latter, now called the Blue Room, seems more likely for it was beautifully decorated to suit the Monroes' elegant taste. The furniture was upholstered in light crimson satin. Matching taffeta curtains were draped over a gilt arch centered by a gilded eagle holding an olive branch in one claw and a sheaf of arrows in the other.

The room was lighted by a magnificent crystal and gilt bronze chandelier with 50 candles and entwined with crimson cloth. Sconces in the shape of gilded eagles were on the walls.

Four bridesmaids attended Maria, and Gouverneur's best man was Gen. Thomas A. Jesup, Subsistence Commissary General of the Army.

No one is now sure what Maria wore for her wedding but one nineteenth-century writer speculated it was the handsome gown of white satin with blonde lace that she wore at the New Year's reception in the White House nine months later. Another writer reported that the bride wore a gown of white grosgrain with a long tulle veil, and that Mrs. Monroe wore black velvet and Mrs. Hay wore red velvet, with the coiffures of both matrons highlighted by white ostrich plumes.

Following the ceremony a handsome supper for 42 was served in the dining room. The list of guests was select, composed mostly of family friends.

The splendid carved French bronze-doré plateau, decorated with garlands of fruit and vines with figures of Bacchus and Bacchantes, and reflecting 60 candles in its large, oval mirror, was on display in all its grandeur. So were the other magnificent gilt bronze pieces the President had ordered from France—

candlesticks and fruit baskets and vases enhanced by a glittering glow, for the dining room was lighted with imported French lamps.

Also furnishing the Executive Mansion were many fine pieces of furniture typical of the graceful, elegant Louis XVI period, bought by Monroe when he was Minister to France. When Monroe was elected President, the mansion was almost empty, having been thoroughly sacked by the British during the war. The new President moved his own furniture in, and it graced the White House throughout his administration. Many of these furnishings, together with other Monroe mementoes, are now on display in the James Monroe Memorial Library in Fredericksburg, Virginia.

The evening following the wedding, Secretary of State and Mrs. Adams dined at Colonel Taylor's and "heard a great talk of the wedding, and as usual many ill-natured remarks. A person in public office in this country is very much in the situation of the man in the fable who endeavoring to please everybody entirely failed. In all things which do not concern the public I am very much inclined to do as I please and I think the P. [President] should so, too, for his own comfort . . ." Louisa wrote in her diary.

"There are to be two drawing rooms Monday and Tuesday next . . . I mentioned that the corps diplomatique were not to be admitted on the occasion to the ladies and they were all excessively shocked."

After a three-day wedding trip, the Gouverneurs returned to a full calendar of social events celebrating their marriage. It began with the two White House drawing rooms. At both, President and Mrs. Monroe mingled with the guests while Maria received as hostess of the mansion.

The Adamses attended the first one, which was "very thin in the consequence of bad weather." The President shook hands with Mrs. Adams, to her surprise, for this was still the era of bowing.

News of the death of the British King George III and the Duke of Kent had just arrived from Europe. And it was whispered that Gouverneur, who was then private secretary to the President, was to be sent to Europe on a foreign mission as a minister.

"The bride was attended by her bridesmaids, four in number, all very pretty girls," said Louisa Adams. "I didn't get a bit of cake and Mary had none to dream on ... So much for this *little great affair* which has occasioned so much talk and so much ill nature."

That Mrs. Adams blamed Eliza for much of the talk and troubles is evident from this description in her diary:

"This woman is made up of so many great and little qualities, is so full of agreables and disagreables, so accomplished and so ill bred, has so much sense and so little judgment that she altogether is so proud and so mean I scarcely ever met such a compound.

"But of one striking trait I can pronounce, and that is her love of scandal, no reputation is safe in her hands and I *never* since the first moment of my acquaintance with her have heard her speak well of any human being."

The honor of giving the first ball—just nine days after the wedding—went to the great Naval hero Commodore Stephen Decatur and his wife. The carriages rolled up to the red brick Decatur house, the first private house erected on Lafayette Square. Invitations to the Decaturs' brilliant balls were sought after, and the cream of Washington society turned out to honor the newlyweds Samuel and Maria Gouverneur.

But the handsome Commodore appeared distracted and out of spirits at the gala party. The guests formed a semicircle around Mrs. Decatur, who played the harp, and Decatur himself stood in the center of the semicircle gazing devotedly at his wife. He turned to his good friend and confidant, Commodore David Porter, who was planning a ball to honor the Gouverneurs the following week, and said: "I may spoil your party."

For Decatur had accepted the challenge to a duel with Commodore James Barron for the following Wednesday morning.

The ball guests included the Misses Douglas of New York, who were granddaughters of the Scotsman who was private tutor to President Monroe when he was a boy. Eliza Hay was not there, for she was taking her turn sitting with the John C. Calhouns' child, who was seriously ill and not expected to live.

On Tuesday the Adamses entertained in the ballroom of their home. The Secretary of State noted the occasion in his diary: "This evening the party at our house was crowded; about one hundred persons. Mrs. Adams made it a sort of wedding party to the new married couple Mr. and Mrs. Gouverneur. They danced cotillions and it was near midnight when the company left us."

Decatur had been prescient. The following day—Wednesday, March 22—he lay dead, having been fatally wounded in the duel at Bladensburg with Commodore Barron.

The cause of the duel was a long-standing hostility between the two men. Decatur had sat on the court martial in 1807 that had suspended Barron's Naval commission for five years for mishandling an incident on his ship. Barron then went to Europe. War broke out before the five years were up, and Barron remained in Europe, returning to the United States in 1818, when he applied to be reinstated in the Navy.

Decatur condemned Barron for not returning from abroad to fight for his country in the war and it was said Decatur blocked Barron's reinstatement in the Navy, which led to bitter correspondence and eventually the challenge.

Legend has it that as the two men lay on the ground side by side after the duel, Decatur dying and Barron wounded, Decatur asked: "Why did you not return to America when war broke out?" and that Barron replied that he had not had the money to pay his way home.

Decatur was taken to his Lafayette Square home, where he died that evening. Congress adjourned for his funeral, which was held two days later. Invitations to the parties honoring the Gouverneurs by the Porters and the family of Albertina Van Ness, one of Maria's bridesmaids, were immediately withdrawn as the shocked nation mourned its great hero, "one who has illuminated history and given grace and dignity to its character in the eyes of the world," a saddened Secretary Adams wrote in his diary.

Mrs. William Winston Seaton, wife of the editor of the *National Intelligencer*, wrote to a friend about those momentous days in March.

". . . The New York style was adopted at Maria Monroe's wedding. Only the attendants, the relations, and a few old friends of the bride and groom witnessed the ceremony, and the bridesmaids were told that their company and services would be dispensed with until the following Tuesday, when the bride would receive visitors. Accordingly all who visit at the President's paid their respects to Mrs. Gouverneur, who presided in her mother's place on this evening, while Mrs. Monroe mingled with the other citizens. Every visitor was led to the bride and introduced in all form. But the bridal festivities have received a check which will prevent any further attentions to the President's family, in the *murder* of Decatur! The first ball, and which we attended, consequent on the wedding, was given by the Decaturs! Invitations were out from Van Ness, Commodore Porter, etc., all of which were remanded on so fatal a catastrophe to the man identified with the glorious success of his country in the late war . . . Commodore Barron lies ill, but not dangerously wounded. The explanation which took place *after* the recontre, and before they were removed from the ground, would have prevented it. They repeated to each other that they harbored no enmity, and hoped to meet, better friends, in another world."

Unlike her domineering sister Eliza, Maria was a quiet girl who was fond of books and writing poetry but was also an accomplished horsewoman. Born in Virginia in April 1802, while her father was Governor of the Commonwealth, she was 15 years younger than Eliza.

Before Maria could talk, her parents took her to France, where her father was sent to negotiate the Louisiana Purchase. By the time she was 5, Maria and her family were back in the United States and it is said the elegant Mrs. Monroe's little daughter introduced the latest French juvenile fashion, pantalettes, to this country.

A prominent citizen of Williamsburg, St. George Tucker, met Colonel Monroe and his family on their return from France and described little Maria in a letter:

". . . Your Mama has referred you to me for an account of little Maria Monroe, who is I believe a few months older than our darling Fannilea. She was dressed in a short frock that reached about half way between her knees and ankles, under which she displayed a long pair of loose pantaloons. I was so pleased with it and so persuaded that you would immediately adopt it for Fannilea that I took more than ordinary notice of it. The little girl did not fail to evince the advantages of her dress. She had a small spaniel dog, with whom she was continually engaged in a trial of skill, and the general opinion seemed to be that she turned and twisted about more than the spaniel. At intervals, when she had tired the dog she was bestriding first Mama's, then her sister's, then her Papa's knees and then again the spaniel, till we left the room. I must recommend her dress for my dear brats."

Samuel Gouverneur, her cousin, was private secretary to the President and lived in the Executive Mansion for nearly two years before he and Maria became engaged. Monroe gave his consent to the marriage and Gouverneur presented his young finance with a rose-cut diamond ring in a gold setting.

Samuel was the son of Mrs. Monroe's sister, Hester Kortright, who had married the wealthy and socially prominent Nicholas Gouverneur of New York. The youngest and most beautiful Kortright sister, Elizabeth (Maria's mother), had accepted an unknown country lawyer from Virginia, Rep. James Monroe. They were married over the bitter oppositon of her father, Captain Lawrence Kortright, an aristocrat and former British Army officer whose sympathies were with the King during the Revolution.

Kortright did not consider the plain and awkward Monroe a promising match for his beautiful daughter, and Elizabeth, herself, had a distant air that made her appear haughty in contrast to Monroe's kind, unpretentious manner.

When the Monroes left the White House in 1825, Maria and Gouverneur moved with them to Oak Hill, the Monroe plantation in Loudoun County, Virginia, and later went on to New York City, where Gouverneur served as Postmaster. The couple had four children, James Monroe, Elizabeth, Samuel L. and a daughter who died in infancy.

Among the wedding gifts were a set of sterling silver flatware and a pair of Sheffield silverplate candlesticks from the President and Mrs. Monroe.

On more than one occasion the family silver was saved by Maria's ingenuity. Her husband, a man of splendid tastes and much charm, had his ups and downs financially because of a weakness for cards and horses. During the down period, he would sell anything he could to raise money.

Maria often hid the silver from her husband. Years later, their son, Samuel L. Gouverneur, Jr., said his father often said to him, "Son, for God's sake, get your mother to bring the silver out, because we're going to have guests for dinner."

The candlesticks, in the Adam style resembling classical columns, feature the Gouverneur crest and are embossed with garlands and beaded trim. They are now in the James Monroe Memorial Library.

In his will, President Monroe left his Oak Hill estate, including the French furniture that had graced the White House, to Maria. She, in turn, willed all her possessions to her husband when she died at Oak Hill in 1850.

Gouverneur later married Mary Digges Lee of Frederick County, Maryland, and on his death left everything to his second wife. Maria's son Samuel contested the will and won, and the Monroe heirlooms went to Maria's descendants. Many are on display in the Monroe Library at Fredericksburg, Virginia.

Quotations from the Adams Papers are from the microfilm edition, by permission of the Massachusetts Historical Society.

The Sheffield Plate Candlesticks were wedding gifts of President and Mrs. James Monroe to Maria. They are in the James Monroe Memorial Library in Fredericksburg, Virginia. The Punch Bowl (probably Spanish) was originally the Monroe's, presented to them while in Europe. It is now owned by Maria's descendant, Laurence Hoes.

III

The President's Son Marries

Mary Catherine Hellen - John Adams, II
February 25, 1828

he only President's son to be married in the White House during its 166-year history was John Adams II, son of President and Mrs. John Quincy Adams. He was married on February 25, 1828, to his cousin Mary Catherine Hellen. (John Quincy Adams had married Louisa Catherine Johnson while his father was President, but in London on July 27, 1797.)

The courtship of young John Adams and Mary Hellen is the fascinating tale of three Adams brothers who were in love with their coquettish cousin. Historically it is told from the point of view of the men and their mother, as recorded in the diaries and letters of the articulate Adams family.

Mary Hellen's own point of view is still a mystery. Adams historians are hopeful that when the diary of young Abigail Adams—Mary's cousin and confidante during her stormy romances—is found it may give a clue to Mary's side of the family intrigue.

Some nineteenth-century chroniclers had access to Abby's diary and a few delightful anecdotes describing the wedding of Mary and John have survived through passages quoted by them.

Mary's flirtatious ways eventually prejudiced more than one of the Adams family against her. The impact she had on the Adams brothers was best expressed by the youngest, Charles Francis. In his diary he called her "one of the most capricious women that were ever formed in a capricious race."

Mary was the orphaned daughter of Mrs. Adams's sister, Nancy Johnson Hellen, and her husband, Walter Hellen, Jr. She was mothered by Louisa Catherine Adams, as were Johnson and Thomas J. Hellen, the other two children of this couple. Mary lived in the White House throughout the Adams adminis-

Mary Catherine Hellen who won the love of President John Quincy Adams's three sons and married one of them in the White House.

tration. She was a young beauty with a peaches and cream complexion, hazel eyes and shining brown hair.

It was of 13-year-old Mary Catherine Hellen that Louisa Catherine was thinking when she came away empty handed from the White House reception for Maria Monroe Gouverneur and Samuel Lawrence Gouverneur just a few days after their wedding in 1820.

"I didn't get a bit of cake and Mary had none to dream on," lamented Louisa, the wife of Secretary of State Adams.

But Mary didn't need wedding cake to put romantic dreams into her head. She had a few of her own.

First object of Mary's flirtatious attentions was Charles Francis, who was Mary's age and still living at home while his older brothers, George and John, were attending Harvard.

Little cousin Abby was also living in the family circle, and the three cousins shared favorite books and an occasional evening at the theater.

Mrs. Adams was a leading hostess in the Capital. She spoke French fluently, having lived in France until she was 7, and her "drawing rooms" were a delightful mixture of American hospitality and old-world sophistication. Diplomats felt at home in her parlor, and with her many talents—she played the harp and the spinet, sketched and wrote—found her a most interesting and pleasant person.

She was hostess at a splendid party in honor of the Hero of New Orleans, General Andrew Jackson, in January 1824.

For the grand ball, all the rooms of the big double house on F Street were entwined with greens and roses "and lighted with small glass variegated lamps and a lustre in the center which produced a beautiful effect," Abby noted in her diary. She and Mary spent a week making decorations for the party. On the floor of the ballroom were chalk paintings of the American eagle and flags and the words, "Welcome to the Hero of New Orleans."

Mary and Abby shared with their cousins John and Charles Francis the excitement of the evening, watching Aunt Louisa receive the distinguished guests with General Jackson standing by her side. So brilliant was the ball, a long poem commemorating the event was published in the *National Journal*. It said, in part:

"Wend your way with the world tonight—

. . . .

Belles and matrons, maids and madames
Are all gone to Mrs. Adams' . . ."

Missing out on the fun was George Washington Adams, the oldest son, who had graduated from Harvard and was in Boston reading law in Daniel Webster's office.

Secretary of State Adams was ever concerned that all three of his sons had "not only their own honor but that of two preceding generations to sustain." And he was especially ambitious for George to have a distinguished career befitting his illustrious name. George was both brilliant and charming, and though he chose law as his profession, he thought "literature is too delightful to be abandoned" and still wrote a bit of poetry on the side.

To Mary, George was the dashing "older man" in the Adams trio of sons, and when he came to Washington on frequent visits, she enjoyed charming him, too.

Mary's delightful ways enraptured George, like Charles Francis before him, and by mid-summer 1823 George asked his father's consent to their engagement.

When Adams asked his eldest son how long he expected the engagement to Mary to be prolonged, he was told "perhaps five or six years, till his prospects would warrant his marrying." To this, the father gave his conditional consent to the engagement.

When Mary became engaged to George, Charles Francis was crushed and could not shake off his infatuation for his capricious cousin.

"I had a dream . . . for it could have been nothing else, and such as it was, I never expect similar happiness again," he confided in his diary about his first love for Mary, long after the romantic connection was broken off.

Mary apparently still enjoyed her power over Charles Francis's affections whenever he returned home during vacations from Harvard, where he was an undergraduate while George was studying law with Mr. Webster in Boston.

"She has some alluring ways which are apt to make every man forget himself," Charles Francis wrote in his diary, adding, "George . . . would be in a perfect fever and sickness if he

33

was to imagine that she had encouraged·me in the least."

Mary probably tried to be true to George. And when George wrote—which wasn't often—he penned affectionate letters to his betrothed.

But George was too far away to hold the volatile affection of Mary, and the temptation to flirt with her good-looking cousin John was too much for the fickle Mary to resist.

John, the second son, was living in Washington, studying law under his father's guidance, after being expelled from Harvard for participating in the great student rebellion of 1823. Even the persuasive powers of the Secretary of State could not get his son reinstated in Harvard College.

John was the handsomest of the trio of sons, but there was about him, at times, "an affected mystery which repels all the good feelings of the heart, the more unfortunate as it is not known by himself to produce the effects which it does," as he was once described by Charles Francis.

While the romance between John and Mary was warming up in Washington, the two Massachusetts-based brothers met frequently. Charles Francis, the youngest of the three brothers but the wiser from experience, suspected the worst but tried not to say too much to George.

By August, the rumblings of family dissension in Washington reached Charles Francis in Massachusetts.

"There is something going on in Washington to the bottom of which I cannot see. And I receive dark and mysterious hints about the matter in every letter upon the subject of family affairs. George is concerned and, for all I know, John, but it is certain I have no connection with the matter. I have suffered too much already. John writes with a little bitterness and my Mother with considerable. . . . " he noted quizzically in his diary.

The mystery cleared in September, when the Adams clan gathered in Quincy for dinner with old John Adams—who at 89 was very deaf, yellow in complexion, weak in voice. Charles Francis and his mother managed a private conversation, which confirmed young Adams's suspicions.

"Of one thing I am satisfied, that Mary has been behaving unworthily to George and consequently that if he marries her, he connects himself with a woman who has no personal affection for him. . . . My Mother is half inclined to the marriage and half opposed, my Father tacitly opposed. . . . I am sorry for John who, I understand, is the victim of her arts, partially, as it is a conflict in his high feelings of honor which should have been spared him. But I am confident absence will cure him at almost any time. . . . "

But the magic cure-all for infatuations which Charles Francis prescribed—absence—was not to come about.

Mary Catherine Hellen moved into the White House with the rest of the Adams family in March 1825, when John Quincy Adams became President—after a tight race with the Hero of New Orleans, General Jackson, that had thrown the election decision into the House of Representatives.

Young John became private secretary for his father the President, and father and son were closer than they had ever been before, frequently slipping off together for a swim across the Potomac in the early morning hours.

Within the White House walls, John's courtship of Mary continued along its inevitable way. And the warm, open relationship that John and Charles Francis once enjoyed disappeared.

Mrs. Adams, who was quite aware of the latest romance blossoming in her home, came to the President on November 20, 1827, and "proposed to me that John and Mary should be married this day fortnight," the President noted in his diary. After thinking it over for a few days, the President could not bring himself to "consent to the marriage of John and Mary Hellen at this time."

The engagement was an off-again, on-again affair, and Mrs. Adams announced the news of the wedding date—set by John for February 25, 1828—in a letter to Charles Francis with the terse comment: "I have declined having anything to do with it, therefore can give you no further information."

Mrs. Adams did come to the Monday evening ceremony in the oval drawing room, furnished with the elegant light crimson satin-covered furniture President Monroe had ordered made in France and the beautiful bronze-doré Minerva clock gracing the mantelpiece. But neither George nor Charles Francis attended the marriage ceremony or the festivities following the wedding day.

The Rev. William Hawley of St. John's Church on Lafayette Square, in his old-fashioned knee breeches and silver shoe buckles, performed the Episcopal ceremony before the President and Mrs. Adams, Abby Adams, Judge William Cranch and his daughter Elizabeth, Edward Everett, Mr. and Mrs. Frye and their son Thomas, Johnson and Thomas J. Hellen, Dr. Henry Huntt, Columbus and Frances Munroe, Matilda Pleasonton, George and Sophia Ramsay, Tench Ringgold, Mary Roberdeau, Mr. and Mrs. W. S. Smith, Dr. Watkins and his son William, and the servants of the family.

"The bride looked very handsome in white satin, orange blossoms and pearls," wrote Abby, who was one of the four bridesmaids. Four groomsmen attended John.

The bridesmaids had an amusing time hanging garlands of flowers and ribbons in the oval drawing room with the groomsmen. There was a supper following the ceremony and the bridesmaids "passed the cake through the ring" and cut slices for the wedding guests to take home.

"The company retired about midnight. May the blessing of God almighty rest upon this union," concluded the President's diary for the wedding day.

First Lady Louisa Catherine was "quite unwell" the following day. But she did manage to take pen in hand to write a letter to Charles Francis in Cambridge, and send along a piece of wedding cake.

To her youngest son, who had been the first to fall for Mary's charms, Louisa wrote:

"You will observe by the tone of my letter to Abby [Brooks, Charles Francis's fiancée] that I am not much in a humour to write. I shall therefore only announce to you the fact that the wedding is over, that Madame is cool easy and indifferent as ever and that John looks already as if he had all the cares in the world upon his shoulders and my heart tells me that there is much to fear—

"In consequence of Gen'l Brown's funeral which is to go immediately from our house the young couple will not see company until Thursday and I am very glad of it as John looks quite sick. . . . I send you a piece of cake as it is the fashion. Judge Cranch declined taking any as he said old people had 'nothing but dreams' on such occasions.

"Adieu. Come on with George I entreat you if it is possible for your mutual visit will restore harmony to the family and we shall all be happy and none so much as your affectionate mother, L.C. Adams."

It was General-of-the-Army Brown's funeral that postponed the reception until Thursday. But Louisa was no better Thursday, the day of the reception, and "Dr. Huntt was with her three times in the day."

In his diary for Thursday, February 28, the President recorded: "A multitude of other visitors called on the new married couple of our family—and Columbus and Frances Munroe, William Watkins, Thomas J. Hellen, George Ramsay and Matilda Pleasonton the bridesmaids and groomsmen of the wedding dined with us." There was a gay reception in the beautiful yellow drawing room—now the Red Room—and the dignified President joined in the dancing of the Virginia Reel.

"It was one of the pleasantest days I ever passed," Abby girlishly wrote of the event.

On December 2, 1828, a daughter was born to John and Mary in the White House, and the arrival of little Mary Louisa —the President's first grandchild—was a joyous time for the President and Louisa Catherine as well as the proud parents.

But the family reconciliation Louisa hoped for was not to come about for some time—and then under tragic circumstances.

George was still in Boston, leading a lone existence, and was in a rundown condition both physically and mentally. He retained his charm throughout his ups and downs, but unfortunately became a drunkard and mismanaged family financial interests.

On the way to a visit with his parents in April 1829— which he probably anticipated would mean a confrontation with his father about his misdeeds—on board the "Benjamin Franklin" en route from Providence to New York, George became deranged and either jumped or fell overboard.

The grief over the calamity of George's death brought his parents closer together and did much to bring about the family reconciliation and to soften the bitter feelings between the remaining brothers, John and Charles Francis.

John Quincy Adams left the White House in March 1829, but maintained a residence in Washington. Young John also stayed on in Washington to practice law. When the bank was about to foreclose on the heavily mortgaged Columbian Mills that belonged to a cousin of Louisa, John Quincy Adams came to the rescue and bought the mills, and John took over the management. He succeeded in getting the business—now named the Adams Mill—out of the red. And, with the financial help of his father, John built a home on Sixteenth Street between I and K Streets, just two blocks from the White House.

A second daughter was born to John and Mary in 1830, and they named her Georgianna Frances, the feminine version of her two uncles' names. The arrival of the two little daughters in young John's family did wonders in helping smooth over the strained family relations of the past.

But the business was a millstone, literally, around the necks of both John and his father for the rest of their lives. Adams Mill Road, named for the old mill which has long been in ruins, is the one existing reminder of this miserable business, which sapped both the finances and energies of the former President and his son.

John's health failed, and his father begged him to leave Washington's unhealthful climate and move to Quincy, where he could manage the Adams estate. But it was too late: John died on October 23, 1834, at the age of 31.

"A more honest soul, or more tender heart never breathed on the face of this earth," his grief-stricken father wrote in his diary.

Mary and the two little girls moved into the old Adams home on F Street with John Quincy Adams and his wife. Sadness came to the family again in 1839 when Georgianna Frances died at the age of nine.

Her grandparents adored Mary Louisa, who brought great happiness into their lives, for she and her mother made their permanent home with the former President and Mrs. Adams.

Mary Hellen Adams lived until 1870, surviving even her daughter Mary Louisa, who died in childbirth. In 1873, John and his Harvard classmates received their degrees, bestowed posthumously by the Harvard Corporation.

Excerpts reprinted by permission of the publishers from *The Diary of Charles Francis Adams*, Aida and David Donald, editors, Cambridge, Mass.:

The Belknap Press of Harvard University Press, c 1964 Massachusetts Historical Society.

Quotations from the diaries and letters of John Quincy Adams, Louisa Catherine Adams and George Washington Adams from the *Adams Papers* are from the microfilm edition and are reprinted by permission of the Massachusetts Historical Society.

John Adams, II, who won Mary Catherine Hellen, the girl his two brothers loved.

George Washington Adams won a promise from Mary Hellen but he lost her in the end.

Charles Francis Adams whose diary told the turbulent love story of John Quincy Adams's three sons.

39

IV

The
Matchmaker's Son
Picks a Bride

Sarah Yorke - Andrew Jackson, Jr.
November 24, 1831

hat romantic old matchmaker Andrew Jackson would have liked to take credit for the three marriages that occurred during one year of his residency in the White House. But the fact is that his fondest effort in that direction misfired, with Cupid proving the truer marksman.

To set the scene, you must know first that President Jackson's wife, Rachel Donelson Jackson, had died a little more than a month before he became President. He spoke of her often and of the happiness they had shared during 37 years of marriage. He wanted all whom they had loved and sheltered during those years to know the same happiness. This included an adopted son, Andrew, Jr., and two girls named Mary.

Mary Eastin was the granddaughter of Rachel Jackson's brother, Colonel John Donelson. She moved into the Donelson mansion after her mother died and was a frequent visitor at the Hermitage, the Jackson home in Nashville. When Gen. Jackson was elected President, he brought Mary to Washington with him.

Mary Anne Lewis had also been taken under the Jacksons' wings after her mother's death. She, too, came to Washington and lived at the White House. In the fall of 1831, she was visiting in New York. Andrew Jackson, Jr., did a great deal of traveling between Washington and Philadelphia and Washington and New York after his foster father became President. The coincidence was too tempting for an old matchmaker to ignore. Gen. Jackson wrote to his son:

"Have you seen Miss Mary Anne Lewis and presented my regards to her? You know that she is a great favorite of mine and that she was also of your dear departed mother. She is a

Sarah Yorke Jackson who married Andrew Jackson, Jr. and went to live in the White House.

Photo by Abbie Rowe, National Park Service,
U. S. Department of the Interior

sweet disposition and I am sure she will make a very fine and elegant woman. It is said here that she is esteemed as one of the belles of New York. I have no doubt that she would make a sweet and affectionate companion."

Perhaps the General laid it on a bit too thick. In any event, Andrew, Jr., had already fallen for someone else in Philadelphia, a demure little Quaker girl known as one of the "three pretty Miss Yorkes."

Sarah Yorke was of distinguished colonial lineage and her father had been a sea captain. She and her two sisters were orphans who had been reared by two aunts. The 20-year-old Andrew met her on one of his Philadelphia trips and late that fall wrote to his father of his intention to marry her. The President replied:

"Since my heavy and irreparable bereavement in the death of my dear and ever to be lamented wife, the only object that makes life desirable to me is to see you happy and prosperous and permanently settled in life, united to an amiable wife of respectability, one whose disposition and amiable qualities are calculated to make you happy. . . .

"You say that Sarah possesses every quality necessary to make you happy. The amiability of her temper and her other good qualities which you represent is a sure pledge to me that she will unite with you in adding to my comfort during life. . . . I shall receive her as a daughter and cherish her as my child."

The wedding was held in Philadelphia on November 24, 1831. The President was unable to attend because of the pressure of state business but sent as his representative the artist Ralph E. W. Earl, who placed on the bride's finger a ring of pearls containing a lock of the President's hair.

The bridal couple went directly from the wedding to the White House, where the President and his official and personal family were waiting in the portico to welcome them. "Look, Sarah," said Andrew, "and see if you can distinguish my father." She replied promptly, "There he is—like Saul among his brethren, head and shoulders above them all!"

The President kissed her, called her "daughter" and conducted her indoors, where he insisted that she sit beside him, saying that he must claim her first for a little while. From that time until she stood beside his deathbed, she filled a daughter's place in his heart.

Sarah Yorke Jackson is described as a beautiful woman with a faultless complexion, black hair and eyes, a lovely figure and an elegant manner. The President said of her: "There was no comparison whatever between her and any other woman I have ever met."

To introduce the bride and bridegroom, the President gave a dinner for about 40 persons, including the Cabinet, and the Diplomatic Corps. Three hundred more guests were invited for music and dancing later in the evening.

The young Jacksons divided the following months between the White House and the Hermitage. Early the following spring, the President wrote his son, "Emily presented Major Donelson [Rachel Jackson's nephew] last night with a fine son. Sarah I hope in due season may present you with a fine daughter—if so I will claim to name it Rachel."

On November 1, 1832, little Rachel was born and 18 months later Andrew Jackson, III, was added to the family. Little Andrew was christened in the White House with members of the Cabinet and the Diplomatic Corps in attendance. Sarah and Andrew had one other son, Samuel.

During the last few months of President Jackson's second term, Sarah and her husband returned to Washington so she could become the official hostess of the mansion. Emily Donelson, who had been the hostess, was too ill to return from Tennessee in the summer of 1836. She died on December 19, 1836.

When President Jackson returned to the Hermitage in March 1837, Sarah and her husband accompanied him. Andrew died in an accident at the close of the Civil War but Sarah lived on at the Hermitage until her death in 1887 at the age of 81.

Sarah Yorke Jackson's beautiful wedding gown of ivory satin and lace, now on display in the First Ladies Hall of the Museum of History and Technology of the Smithsonian Institution.

The Smithsonian Institution

V

Two Brides
Named Mary

Mary Eastin - Lucius Polk
April 10, 1832

Mary Anne Lewis - Alphonse Pageot
November 29, 1832

wo White House weddings took place within one year, 1832, in the Jackson administration. Mary Eastin and Lucius Polk were married on April 10, 1832, and before the year was out, on November 29, wedding bells rang out for Mary Anne Lewis and Alphonse Pageot.

Of all the kith and kin who lived in the White House at one time or another during the Jackson administration, none was dearer to the President than Mary Eastin, granddaughter of Rachel Jackson's brother, Colonel John Donelson.

Little Mary moved into the Donelson mansion after her mother died and she was a frequent visitor at the Jacksons' Hermitage. When the General—now President and a recent widower—brought his official family from Tennessee to the White House, Mary came along.

As a White House resident, the sprightly and personable Mary quickly became a belle, one of her beaux being Major Abram Van Buren, the son of Secretary of State Martin Van Buren. But when she set her cap, she surprised everyone by choosing an English-born naval officer nearly twice her age, Captain Bolton Finch.

He was considered something of a dandy and had been engaged several times previously, but Mary Eastin named February 14, 1832, as an appropriate Valentine's Day wedding date and went to New York to buy her trousseau at Miss Thompson's.

To top off her bridal costume she chose a white satin hat and a wreath of orange blossoms, and also bought a bunch of orange blossoms, probably to adorn her gown. The hat cost $11 and Mary bought a box to keep it in for $1 extra. The

---

Two White House Brides named Mary: Mary Eastin, left, who married Lucius Polk in the White House on April 10, 1832, and Mary Anne Lewis, right, who married Alphonse Pageot on November 29, 1832. This double portrait was painted by artist Ralph Earl, and hangs in Hamilton Place, Columbia, Tennessee.

wreath cost $2 and the additional orange blossoms $1.50.

The extra $1 for the hat box may have been the straw that bent the camel's back, for the President wrote to his friend General John Coffee—Rachel's brother-in-law—asking him to look into his financial prospects.

"I will thank you," he said, "at as early a period as your leisure will permit, to advise me if any and what funds can be collected for me—my son's marriage has increased my expence. The marriage of Mary Eastin, which is to take place the 14th of next month, will add a little more to it, and the conduct of my overseers and the smallness of my present crop will give me nothing from my farm; therefore the desire I have to know all the means I can command and shape expenses accordingly."

The President also described Captain Finch as "a worthy and gallant man but not wealthy, but worthy in every respect, about 40."

Meanwhile, word of the impending nuptials had reached Tennessee. A handsome admirer of Mary, 30-year-old Lucius J. Polk, hitched up a carriage and took off at top speed for Washington prepared to come back with the bride herself.

Lucius was the son of General Jackson's old friend Colonel William Polk, whose friendship with Jackson dated from their youth together in Mecklenburg County, North Carolina. The Polk family was a distinguished one, and grandfather Thomas Polk had received a land warrant for Tennessee territory from the North Carolina Assembly for his services during the Revolutionary War.

Lucius and James K. Polk, who was to become the eleventh President of the United States, were second cousins. Lucius had graduated from the University of North Carolina, then gone to Tennessee to help look after the family's land holdings.

Family history has it that Colonel Polk had won 5000 acres of Tennessee land in a game of chance with the Governor of North Carolina, and this land he divided into tracts of almost 1,300 acres each for Lucius and three other sons.

When Lucius took off from Tennessee, he left plans for the building of a home to which he would bring his bride. His father brought slaves from the old North Carolina estate to Tennessee to make the bricks, cut the timber, and start building a large plantation home.

When the confident suitor arrived in Washington, the President was delighted to see him. Polk is said to have asked the President to plead his cause with Mary, and it is further reported that "Uncle Jackson," as Mary called him, warned her: "Take care, my dear. With love, marriage is heaven; without it, hell."

Whether this weather-beaten bit of philosophy did the trick or not, Mary changed her mind. She called off the Finch wedding and set the date with Lucius for April 10.

Lucius, meanwhile, did all the right things to endear himself to the family. On March 31, just 11 days before his wedding to Mary, he stood as co-sponsor with the President at the baptism of little Andrew Jackson Donelson, son of Andrew Donelson and his wife Emily, who was acting as the official White House hostess for Uncle Andrew.

The Rev. William Hawley, rector of St. John's Church, across the square from the White House, was called on to baptize all the young additions to the Jackson menage, and he was back at the President's on April 10 to perform the Episcopal ceremony uniting Mary and Lucius in matrimony.

However, after Mary's recent about-face with her affections, the President had a few last-minute doubts about whether the new wedding would come off. He wrote to General Coffee: "I believe I may say that Miss Mary Eastin will be married on Tuesday evening next to Mr. Lucius Polk. The guests are all invited and I trust that it will take place."

Lucius J. Polk

The wedding did come off on schedule and the President escorted the 22-year-old bride through the long lemon yellow East Room to the improvised altar.

Jackson had just spent almost $10,000 refurnishing the East Room in a lavish manner. The floor was covered with 500 yards of Brussels carpet in fawn, blue and yellow with a red border, at a cost of $1,058.25. Curtains of blue and yellow moreen were held up by gilded eagles, and gilded stars were emblazoned around the cornice. Over the door were gilded ornamental rays and 24 stars representing the 24 states. Chairs and sofas were covered with blue damask satin. Fine paintings hung on the walls. Around the walls were four pier tables, all with Italian marble tops and richly bronzed and gilded. On each table was a lamp and a pair of French china vases. For this and other state rooms, he had bought as a final touch, 20 spittoons, which cost $12.50 each.

Jackson had also had constructed the North Portico facing Pennsylvania Avenue as his ceremonial entrance, making this side of the mansion the official entrance rather than the south side, which had previously been used for this purpose.

Also as a part of his beautification of the mansion, he planted magnolia trees at the southwest corner in memory of his beloved Rachel. These trees, tall and spreading, still bloom today.

After their East Room wedding, Lucius and Mary set out for a month-long trip to Tennessee. When they arrived, the big house on Lucius's land near Columbia, some 50 miles from Jackson's Hermitage, was well under way. They stayed in Colonel Polk's home near Spring Hill until their own handsome home was completed in late summer of 1832. This they named Hamilton Place and it is still owned by their descendants.

Lucius and Mary Eastin Polk were the parents of 12 children, including two sets of twins. Two sons died at birth and Mary died in childbirth with her second set of twins in 1847 at Hamilton Place. Polk stayed on at Hamilton Place until his death in 1870.

Although Uncle Jackson's first matchmaking scheme for her failed, Mary Anne Lewis also had a White House wedding during the Jackson Administration. She was the daughter of the General's old friend and his quartermaster at New Orleans, Major William Berkeley Lewis.

Mary Anne, one of the motherless children who were taken in by the Jacksons at the Hermitage, was a favorite of Rachel Jackson, and when the General came to Washington he brought Mary Anne and her father with him.

He made her father Second Auditor of the Treasury and let both Mary Anne and her father live at the White House for a time. However criticism from both Jackson's family and official circles of so much official togetherness chased Major Lewis out.

When the General's scheme for a match between his son and Mary Anne didn't work, the old matchmaker thought up another one.

Mary Anne, an 18-year-old beauty, was among those invited to a gay Christmas party at the White House in 1831. One of the guests was Alphonse Pageot, a secretary of the French Legation and the brother of French Minister Serrurier's wife.

Soon after the party Mary Anne and Alphonse Pageot became engaged. The President wished her to have a White House wedding and the date was set for November 29, 1832. Again the East Room was decorated for a wedding, this one the first Catholic ceremony to be held in the President's House.

The Rev. William Matthews of St. Patrick's Catholic Church performed the ceremony before an assembly of family, friends and the Diplomatic Corps. Afterwards the young couple left on a short wedding trip to Philadelphia.

When they returned, they were presented with an elegantly furnished mansion by the bride's father. Major Lewis went with the house, however. He wrote to a friend about his new son-in-law: "I think him an amiable, fine young man, accomplished, well educated and of much promise." He added: "On their return, I shall go to housekeeping with them."

Little Andrew Jackson Pageot was born a year later and was brought over to the White House for his christening by Father Matthews, with the President acting as godfather.

The Pageots moved to France several years later, then returned to Washington where for a short two months during the Polk administration Pageot served as Minister by appointment of the French King. But with the King's overthrow in March 1848, Pageot's function as Minister came to an end.

The Pageots returned to France again and took up residence at Passy (Seine). In November 1866, at the age of 52, Mary Anne died at Avignon unaware that three days earlier her father had died in Nashville, her birthplace.

This 1831 engraving of the White House by H. Brown shows how it looked during the administration of President Andrew Jackson.

49

MRS. MAJOR VAN BUREN
DAUGHTER-IN-LAW OF 8TH PRESIDENT
BY HENRY INMAN, 1842

VI

This Bride Served as First Lady

Angelica Singleton - Abram Van Buren
November 27, 1838

It was love at first sight when Abram Van Buren, eldest son and private secretary of President Martin Van Buren, met Angelica Singleton in the White House in 1837.

The meeting had been arranged by matchmaker Dolley Madison, who wanted her 22-year-old cousin, Angelica, to break up the bachelorhood of the President's four sons, who were then living in the Executive Mansion with their widower father.

The wedding took place on November 27, 1838, at the Singleton home, the Hills near Santee, South Carolina. Beautiful Angelica became the First Lady as President Van Buren's official hostess.

Her background and training fitted her well for this role. She was the daughter of Richard Singleton, a large South Carolina landowner and a member of a family ranked among the bluebloods of the state. She attended a fashionable girls' school in Philadelphia and in 1837 spent a portion of her holiday in Washington.

Although she came to visit her uncle and aunt, Senator and Mrs. William C. Preston, she called also on her cousin "Queen Dolley" Madison, who arranged for her to have a private meeting at the White House with the President and his sons.

The minute he saw her, Abram Van Buren determined to win her for his wife. He had graduated from West Point and had been an Army officer until his father was elected President, when he became his private secretary.

Angelica made her first appearance in her new role on New Year's Day in 1839 and her graciousness during the long hours of standing and receiving guests won much praise.

Angelica Singleton who married Major Abram Van Buren and served as First Lady for her father-in-law, President Martin Van Buren.

Photo by Abbie Rowe, National Park Service
U. S. Department of the Interior

One newspaper, the *Boston Post,* said of that event:

"The Executive Mansion was a place of much more than usual attraction in consequence of the first appearance there of the bride of the President's son and private secretary, Mrs. Abram Van Buren. She is represented as being of rare accomplishments, very modest, yet perfectly easy and graceful in her manners and free and vivacious in her conversation. She was universally admired and is said to have borne the fatigue of a three hours' levee with a patience and pleasantry which must be inexhaustible to last one through so severe a trial."

That reception, however, was one of the rare occasions when the White House was opened to the public during the Van Buren administration. As one of his biographers said, "No longer were the policies of Jefferson, Madison and Monroe observed, and no longer did the public feel free to frequent the President's house whenever they desired, for he abolished the morning receptions and the weekly levees and substituted only one formal levee open to the public on New Year's Day, and no refreshments were offered to his guests, who had to be content to be received at the Executive Mansion and to listen to the Marine Band. That was one cause for bitterness among the Democratic Party leaders—others were the facts that he imported his chef from London, used the rarest of china on his table, and even had gold spoons and a billiard table."

Van Buren, always suave, diplomatic and tactful, did entertain frequently at small but elegant dinners at which he used the gold spoons acquired during President Monroe's day. And the imported chef did provide food that was a great improvement over that of Jackson's day.

Seeing the furniture in a bad state of repair after the heavy use during the Jackson administration, when thousands came to the levees and thought nothing of standing on the chairs if they wished, Van Buren did a thorough renovation and refurnishing of the White House early in his administration.

He auctioned off some of the furniture and spent $25,000 to replace it. He had the furniture in the oval drawing room reupholstered in blue instead of the crimson that had been in use since President Monroe's administration. And the name of the room was then changed to "Blue Room."

Van Buren, who had been a widower for 17 years and had grown accustomed to looking after his own household, personally supervised the interior decoration and approved the addition of glass doors, tinted chinaware and floral carpets.

These seemed ostentatious to a critical public accustomed to the homely hospitality of Jackson's day, but Van Buren wanted only to bring the President's house up to the standards he felt the nation deserved.

Despite his refined manners and high goals, Van Buren was not a popular President with either the public or his Cabinet, whose members thought him unable to cope with the problems of the day. But he was adored by his daughter-in-law, who learned about the President's early life in Kinderhook, New York, where his father was a tavern keeper, from her husband.

At the age of 14, Martin was apprenticed to the one lawyer in the community and stayed with him until he went to another law office for a year of training before opening his own office. He entered politics and went slowly up the ladder. He became Attorney-General of New York, then successively Representative, Senator and Governor of New York. Then he became Vice President in Jackson's second term, a position he resigned to become American Minister to Great Britain, but the Senate refused to confirm his nomination to this post. Then Van Buren was elected to the Presidency with the blessings and support of his predecessor, Andrew Jackson.

Van Buren was temporarily without a hostess in the White House in the spring of 1839 when Angelica and Abram went on a belated bridal trip abroad. Their first stop in London was to visit Angelica's cousin, Andrew Stevenson, who was at that time Minister to Great Britain.

Mrs. Stevenson saw to it that Angelica was presented to Queen Victoria and met all the proper royalty. In Paris, the American Minister, General Cass, presented them to the King and Queen and they were invited to dine at St. Cloud, where Louis Philippe conducted them on a tour of the Palace after dinner.

The two sailed for home to resume their official duties at the White House. Angelica created a sensation at the first levee after her return by receiving the guests from an improvised "throne" on which she sat in a purple velvet dress with a long train. Three long ostrich plumes were in her brown hair, which was parted in the center and fell down her cheeks in corkscrew curls. A pendant held by a rope of pearls decorated her forehead.

As the long line of visitors stared at her with avid curiosity and then passed on to gossip, she sat young, regal and smiling, unaware of the unfavorable impression she was giving.

Many of the guests felt that her appearance was "undemocratic" and that her costume was an example of the President's lavish personal living standards for which the country must pay. The public added Angelica's new ways to the sum total of their dislike for the Van Buren administration.

Angelica's enjoyment of her reign in the White House was marred by the death of her baby girl, who lived only two hours. After the public denied Van Buren the second term he so badly wanted, Angelica and her husband moved to New York City, where she gave birth to three sons, none of whom ever married. She died in 1877, four years after her husband's death on March 15, 1873.

The White House during the Van Buren administration was accented by ornamental iron fences. The Jefferson statue by David d'Angers is now in the rotunda of the Capitol.

VII

Another President's Daughter Marries

Elizabeth Tyler - William Waller
January 31, 1842

lizabeth Tyler, 20-year-old daughter of President and Mrs. John Tyler and affectionately known as "the young princess," was the second Presidential daughter to have a White House wedding. She was married January 31, 1842, to William N. Waller, a young lawyer who had lived next door to the Tylers in Williamsburg, Virginia.

The Rev. William Hawley of St. John's Church, across Lafayette Square from the White House, performed the ceremony in the East Room before Cabinet members and their wives, diplomats and their wives, family friends, including Dolley Madison, and relatives from Virginia.

Mrs. Tyler, who was an invalid, made her only public appearance in the White House at the wedding. A beautiful woman, she had suffered a paralyzing stroke four years earlier and normally kept to her room, quietly knitting with the Bible and a prayer book close at hand.

On the occasion of the wedding, she wore a "perfectly faultless yet unostentatious dress, her face shaded by the soft fine lace of her cap, receiving in her sweet, gentle, self-possessed manner, all the people who were led up and presented to her. She was by far more attractive to me in her appearance and bearing than any other lady in the room, and I believe such was the general impression," wrote her daughter-in-law, Mrs. Robert Tyler, who served as White House hostess.

Of the bride, her sister-in-law wrote:

"Lizzie looked surpassingly lovely in her wedding dress and long blond lace veil, her face literally covered with blushes and dimples. She behaved remarkably well, too; any quantity of compliments were paid to her. I heard one of her bridesmaids express to Mr. [Daniel] Webster her surprise at Lizzie consenting to give up her belleship, with all the delights of Washington society, and the advantages of her position, and retire to a quiet Virginia home.

"'Ah,' he said,

'Love rules the court, the camp, the grove,
'And love is heaven, and heaven is love.' "

Lizzie was already a belle before her father became President. She greatly resembled her mother in both character and beauty, having lovely eyes and complexion and light brown hair that curled down on her neck.

In the White House, she helped her sister-in-law in her duties as hostess. Often at the Saturday afternoon musicals on the South Lawn, Lizzie joined in welcoming the guests and won compliments for her grace and charm.

Her two older sisters were both married and living in Virginia, although they were frequent visitors at the White House and on these visits would appear together in the reception rooms. Mary, the eldest, married at an early age Henry Lightfoot Jones of Charles City County, Virginia, and lived at Woodburn, one of her husband's plantations.

In February 1838, Letitia, the next daughter, married a Mr. Semple and lived at a place called Cedar Hill, a short distance from Williamsburg in New Kent County.

Robert Tyler, the second child and oldest son of the President, was married to Priscilla Cooper, the daughter of Thomas Abthorpe Cooper, the distinguished actor. It was she who served as hostess at the White House for the President in his wife's illness.

The Tylers had four other children. They were John, Tazewell, Alice and one who had died in infancy. Alice married an Episcopal minister years after her father left the White House.

Lizzie tried to live up to the admonition John Tyler gave his children when they moved into the Executive Mansion. He told them:

"Now my children, during the next few years, we are to occupy the home of the President of the United States. I hope you will conduct yourselves with even more than your usual propriety and decorum. Remember you will be much in the public eye. You are to know no favorites. Your visitors will be the citizens of the United States and as such are all to be received with equal courtesy. You will not receive any gifts whatsoever, and allow no one to approach you on the subject of office or favors. These words you will kindly remember, and let it not be incumbent upon me to speak them again."

Public life was not new to the children of John and Letitia Tyler when the family entered the White House. He had served one term as Governor of Virginia, three terms in the House of Representatives, and was twice elected to the Senate before he became Vice-President on the Tippecanoe-and-Tyler-Too ticket headed by William Henry Harrison in 1840. Harrison died only 31 days after taking the Presidential oath and Tyler became President.

Lizzie had many opportunities to display her charm during the nine months she lived in the White House. At a dinner and ball in honor of 23-year-old Prince de Joinville, the third son of Louis Philippe, President Tyler led the way after dinner to the East Room, followed by the Prince and his suite, and the Diplomatic Corps in full court dress. There Elizabeth and the Prince led a *quadrille d'honneur,* after which dancing became general.

Scarcely any notice of Lizzie's wedding appeared in the newspapers of the day because it was considered a private matter. Although there was no reception on the day of the wedding, the White House was thrown open the following evening and a brilliant reception took place.

Many were the gifts Lizzie received. One was a poem written by Maria Monroe Gouverneur, the first daughter of a President to be married in the White House.

Titled "To Miss Tyler on Her Wedding Day," it reads:
The day, the happy day has come
That gives you to your lover's arms;
Check not the tear or rising bloom
That springs from all those strange alarms.

To be a blest and happy wife
Is what all women wish to prove;
And may you know through all your life
The dear delights of wedded love.

To Miss Tyler on her wedding day —

The day, the happy day has come,
That gives you to your lovers Arms;
Check not the tear, or rising bloom,
That springs from all those strange Alarms.

To be a blest and happy wife
Is what all women wish to prove,
And may you know through all your life;
The dear delights of wedded love —

'Tis not strange that you should feel,
Confused in every thought & feeling;
Your bosom heave, the tear should steal;
At thoughts of all the friends you are leaving.

Happy live may your life prove,
All sunshine joy & purest pleasure;
One long, long, day of happy love,
Your husbands joy, his greatest Treasure.

Be to him all that woman ought,
In joy, in health, & every sorrow;
Let his true pleasures, be only sought,
With you to day, With you tomorrow —

Believe not that in halls [...] wealth
'Tis only there that joy you'll find,
As some with friends in your own halls
Theres more content, and peace of mind —

More splendour you may find tis true,
And glitter show and elevation;
But if the world, of you speak true,
You prize not wealth, or this high station —

Your heart's too pure, your mind too high,
To prize the empty pomp and [...]
You leave such scenes without a sigh
To court the joys that on you await —

Lines written to Miss Tyler, daughter of President Tyler on
her wedding day by Maria Hester Monroe, daughter of
President James Monroe subsequently
Mrs. Samuel Laurence Gouverneur

'Tis not strange that you should feel
Confused in every thought and feeling;
Your bosom heave, the tear should steal
At thought of all the friends you're leaving.

Happy girl may your life prove,
All sunshine, joy and purest pleasure;
One long, long day of happy love,
Your husband's joy, his greatest treasure.

Be to him all that woman ought,
In joy and health and every sorrow;
Let his true pleasures be only sought
With you today, with you tomorrow.

Believe not that in palace walls
'Tis only there that joy you'll find;
At home with friends in your own halls
There's more content and peace of mind.

More splendor you may find 'tis true,
And glitter, show, and elevation,
But if the world of you speak true,
You prize not wealth or this high station.

Your heart's too pure, your mind too high,
To prize such empty pomp and state;
You leave such scenes without a sigh
To court the joys that on you wait.

After her wedding, Elizabeth and her husband went to
Williamsburg to live, but she made frequent visits back to the
White House. Eight months later her mother died, clasping in
her hand her favorite flower, the monthly damask rose. Elizabeth had come up from Williamsburg to be with her in her
final illness and was with her at the very end. The following
day, Sunday, the Executive Mansion stood in mourning and
the tolling of the bells of the city announced the sad event. A
funeral was held in the East Room at four o'clock on Monday,
September 12, 1842, and the body returned to the old paternal

residence in New Kent County for interment in the family burial ground.

When her father remarried two years later, Lizzie and her older sisters, Mary and Letitia, found it difficult to accept his 24-year-old bride as a stepmother. But after months of friction, Mary and Elizabeth came to admire the new Mrs. Tyler.

Three months after the wedding, Elizabeth wrote her first letter to her new stepmother and explained her feelings. She said she could not accept Julia as her mother but would try to love her as a sister and expressed hope that the feeling would be reciprocated.

In September of that year, Tyler, who had not been a popular President and had decided not to seek re-election, became concerned over rumors that his son-in-law, William Waller, might support his bitter antagonist Henry Clay as his successor in the White House.

He wrote about it to Elizabeth, saying:

"I am still abused by all the papers in his (Clay's) advocacy, and he urged on that conspiracy in 1841 which was designed to ruin me personally and politically. His opposition to Texas, his attempt to revolutionize the government—through the abolition of the veto power—in short, his total want of principle of every sort renders him the most obnoxious man in the Union. Mr. Polk is, to say the least, a gentleman in principle and conduct. If he comes into power, his administration will be a continuance of my own, since he will be found the advocate of most of my measures. Mr. Clay leads the Federal cohorts; Mr. Polk the Democratic. My friends will be treated with regard and attention, and a rally on their part will secure the election. They have rallied en masse in Pennsylvania, New Jersey, Maryland, Massachusetts, Connecticut, New York, etc. I hope Mr. Waller will seriously ponder before he commits himself to Clay."

After Tyler left the White House Elizabeth visited her father frequently at Sherwood Forest on the James River.

Six years later, or eight years after her marriage, Lizzie died following the birth of her sixth child. Her husband moved to Lynchburg where he became a tobacconist and married his cousin, Jane Meredith Waller, in 1863.

The *Richmond Enquirer* carried the announcement of Lizzie's death:

"Departed this life on June 1, 1850, Mrs. Elizabeth Waller, wife of William Waller, Esq. of Williamsburg, and daughter of Ex-President Tyler. Thus in the bloom of youth, not having reached her 27th year, has one of the loveliest of her sex, lovely in all the attributes that make up the perfect character, the beloved daughter, the adored wife, the Christian mother, descended to the tomb. . . ."

(Actually, she was 28 for the record of her baptism shows she was born in July 1821.)

Lizzie bore six children: William Griffin Waller, Elizabeth Tyler Waller, who died in infancy, John Tyler Waller, Letitia Waller, who died in infancy, Mary Stuart Waller and Robert Tyler Waller, who was born on May 17 before his mother's death on June 1.

William went to West Point but resigned during the Civil War and married the youngest sister of the wife of Jefferson Davis in the Executive Mansion of the Confederate States in Richmond. He later became assistant editor of the *Savannah News* and managing editor of the *Richmond Times*.

John died in ambush during the Civil War fighting, as he termed it, "for my mother's grave." Mary Stuart was married on April 25, 1867, in St. Paul's Church in Lynchburg, to Louis Gourdin Young of Charleston, South Carolina. Robert married Emily Greene Johnson at Savannah, Georgia, on December 19, 1878. He died at Savannah on August 9, 1920.

The White House as it looked during the administration of President John Tyler.

VIII

President Tyler
Takes a Bride

Julia Gardiner - John Tyler
June 26, 1844

John Tyler was the first President to be married while in office. His bride was the beautiful New York socialite Julia Gardiner, who had left a trail of broken romances in Rome, Paris, London, New York and Washington.

The marriage of the 54-year-old widower President to the 24-year-old Julia on June 26, 1844, in New York was the talk of the young nation—not all of it favorable talk. John Quincy Adams, then 77, termed it a "January-May" wedding and wrote in his diary: "Capt. Tyler and his bride are the laughingstock of this city. It seems as if he was racing for a prize banner to the nuptials of the mock-heroic—the sublime to the ridiculous."

Julia met President Tyler at a White House reception several months before the death of his first wife. She went with her father and her current beau, Richard R. Waldron, a Navy purser.

She recalled later that the President "welcomed us with an urbanity which made the deepest impression upon my father, and we could not help commenting as we left the room upon the silvery sweetness of his voice, that seemed in just attune with the incomparable grace of his bearing and the elegant ease of his conversation."

Tyler was tall and slender, with light brown hair and piercing blue eyes. He paid her such lavish compliments that the people around them in the Green Room stopped and listened. This was just 11 days before the President gave his 20-year-old daughter Elizabeth's hand in marriage to William Waller, a Williamsburg tobacco planter and writer, at a grand wedding in the East Room.

Julia Gardiner, later Mrs. John Tyler, shocked her neighbors in 1840 when she posed for this testimonial advertisement for a New York department store which called her "The Rose of Long Island." The rare color lithograph, now considered a very early and unique example of class advertising, is in the collections of the Museum of the City of New York. The placard Julia carries reads: "I'll purchase at Bogert and Mecamly's. . . . Their goods are beautiful and astonishingly cheap."

Courtesy Museum of the City of New York

There is no record of Julia having been at that wedding, but she was to be a frequent guest at the White House later.

Social events at the White House during the Tyler Administration were brilliant affairs. Even John Quincy Adams was complimentary in his comments on the entertaining done by the President, whose daughter-in-law, Mrs. Robert Tyler, served as his hostess. After attending a party at the White House in June of that year, Adams said that the courtesies they paid their guests were all that the accomplished European courts could have displayed.

Letitia Christian Tyler, the President's first wife, was an invalid as a result of a paralytic stroke four years earlier and left the hostess responsibilities to her daughter-in-law. She made her only public appearance at the White House at Elizabeth's wedding. Eight months after the wedding, Mrs. Tyler died quietly in her room. The President, who had been deeply devoted to her, went into mourning.

Three months later, in December 1842, gay, sophisticated Julia Gardiner and her parents came to Washington for their second social season. Julia had already had a gay whirl in the elite circles of New York and in Rome, Paris and London, where her parents took her and her younger sister, Margaret, for a season.

In every capital, Julia found romance. Crossing the English Channel to France, her charm captivated one of the passengers, a titled Englishman; in Rome, she flirted with a young German nobleman visiting there; in London, it was an employee of the War Ministry.

They were in Italy in the spring of 1841 when they heard of the death of President Harrison and the accession to the Presidency of John Tyler. Both daughters draped their left wrist in black crepe to testify the sense of grief felt by Americans for the death of the "Hero of Tippecanoe."

When they returned home via Paris, Julia brought with her a yellow canary, which she named Johnny Ty for the new president.

A petite five foot, three inches, with an hourglass waist, Julia was a real beauty. She had large gray eyes, raven hair parted in the middle with a bun over each ear and a clear

THE PRESIDENT'S BRIDE.

olive complexion. Her irrepressible personality kept her family wondering what she would do next.

She had attended a fashionable girls' school in New York and after graduating found the social life in East Hampton slightly boring. In 1840 she shocked her parents and their East Hampton neighbors when she posed for a testimonial advertisement of a New York department store which called her "the Rose of Long Island." The ad pictured her with a dandy, and on her arm was a purse with the placard: "I'll purchase at Bogart and Mecamly's . . . Their goods are beautiful and astonishingly cheap." Actually, the Gardiners patronized a store considered much more exclusive.

Julia came from an old New York family whose founder was Lion Gardiner. He immigrated to New York in 1635 and later settled on Gardiner's Island, which he purchased from the Indians. Julia's father, David Gardiner, was a former New York State Senator who enjoyed mingling with legislators and politicians. Her mother was the daughter of Michael McLachlin, a rich New York merchant.

When the Gardiners arrived in Washington, they took quarters at Mrs. Peyton's boarding house on the corner of Pennsylvania Avenue and Four-and-a-Half Street. It had been recommended to them by their old friend, Arthur Middleton of South Carolina, then Minister to Madrid.

Here the Gardiner girls' popularity quickly exceeded the capacity of the landlady's parlor and they had to take a private parlor to entertain their guests. Julia flirted with Senators, Representatives and Supreme Court Justices, who vied with each other for the distinction of being her escort.

Although the Capital was in mourning for the President's dead wife, Julia and her sister were invited to the White House by Priscilla Tyler, the President's daughter-in-law, for "a quiet game of whist," and Julia was asked to bring her guitar and play. The President was an accomplished violinist, as well as being a poet.

That winter she flirted with the President's son, John Tyler, Jr., a frequent caller at the Gardiners'. Her charm and beauty had also caught the admiring eyes of the widower President, who was not unmindful of the other attentions focused on her.

JOHN TYLER of VIRGINIA,
10th PRESIDENT,
April 6,1841 to March 4,1845.

President John Tyler who courted a 24-year-old New York socialite in the White House and then brought her there as his bride after a wedding in New York.

69

Washington April 20. 1844

I have the permission of your dear daughter Miss Julia Gardiner, to ask your approbation of my addresses to her, dear Madam, and to obtain your consent to our marriage which in all dutiful obedience she refers to your decision. May I indulge the hope that you will see in this nothing to object, and that you will confer upon me the high privilege of reb-ututing yourself in all that care and atten-tion which you have so affectionately bes-towd upon her. My position in Society will I trust serve as a guarantee for the assurance which I give, that it will be the study of my life to advance her happiness by all and every means in my power.

I pray you Madam to be assured of my highest regard and esteem.

John Tyler

Mrs Gardiner.

This is the letter John Tyler wrote Mrs. David Gardiner asking permission to marry her daughter Julia Gardiner. It is among the Gardiner family papers in the Yale University Library.

Representative Francis W. Pickens, a 37-year-old South Carolina widower with four children, was one of her persistent suitors. He asked her to marry him. So did 57-year-old Supreme Court Justice John McLean. Both were rejected, but gently and adroitly, so she could use their attentions to further her friendship with President Tyler.

Julia made many visits to the White House, ostensibly to see the President's daughter-in-law. She invariably also saw the President. Her sister Margaret wrote of one occasion when he kissed Margaret's hand and was "proceeding to treat Julia in the same manner when she snatched away her hand and flew down the stairs with the President after her around the chairs and tables until at last he caught her. It was truly amusing."

By mid-February, five months after his first wife's death, Tyler had decided to marry Julia. At a George Washington's Birthday Ball in the White House, he took her on a private stroll through the rooms and proposed to her. Julia, not yet ready to let him catch her, replied "No, no, no," shaking her head each time and flinging the dangling tassle on her crimson Greek cap into the President's face.

Recalling the event years later, she said, "It amused me to see the expression on his face as he tried to make love to me and the tassle brushed his face."

Tyler might have been discouraged but he didn't give up. He continued to see Julia whenever possible. On March 15, he spoke of marriage again, this time in Margaret's presence. Again there was no consent, although her family was pleased with the news and also flattered at the attention the President was paying their daughter.

Before the Gardiners left Washington later that month to return to Long Island, Tyler again proposed to Julia. This time her mother intervened and insisted that he let her daughter wait a few months to be sure of her feelings. But there was a strong feeling between Julia and the President when they parted.

Tyler's letters to her that summer were filled with romantic sentiments that somehow got to be the talk of East Hampton. The two did not see each other again, however, until Gardiner and his two daughters returned to Washington in February 1844. This time Mrs. Gardiner stayed behind because of illness.

Three days after their arrival they attended a levee at the White House and the following day the Gardiners were among 300 persons who accompanied the President on an excursion down the Potomac River aboard the Navy's new steam frigate *Princeton*.

The catastrophe which occurred on that occasion was described years later by Julia in an interview with Nellie Bly and published in the *New York World* and other papers. It follows in part:

"On the 28th of February Commodore Stockton gave a party on the Potomac. Everybody was there, and we had a lovely time. I was with my father when a gentleman came to me and said 'Miss Gardiner, the President wishes to take you into the collation which is just served.' 'I suppose I will have to obey orders,' I replied with a laugh and asking my father to follow me, I started down. Just then the wind caught my veil and blew it up. Father caught it with his cane and brought it down, saying, 'Take care of your streamer!' They were almost the last words I ever heard him speak. When we got down the President seated me at the head of the table with him, and he handed me a glass of champagne. Father was standing just back of my chair so I handed the glass over my shoulder saying, 'Here, Pa!' He did not take it, but he said, 'My time will soon come.' He meant his time to be served but the words have always seemed prophetic to me. That moment some one called down for the President to come up and see the latest shot fired, but he said he would not go as he was better engaged. My father started with some other gentlemen.

"Just then we heard the shot and the smoke began to come down the companionway. 'Something must be wrong,' I said to the young man [seated on the other side of her] and he started up to see. He got to the door and turned around and gave me such a look of horror that I shall never forget it. That moment I heard someone say, 'The Secretary of State is dead!' I was frightened and I tried to get upstairs. 'Something has happened. Let me go to my father,' I cried, but they kept me back.

"Someone told me that there had been an accident, the gun had exploded, but that there was such a crowd that it would do no good for me to try to get there. I was told then that he was wounded. That drove me frantic. I begged them to let me go and help him, that he loved me and would want me near him. One lady, seeing my agony, said 'My dear child, you can do no good. Your father is in heaven.'

"'Yes,' Mrs. Tyler [Julia] continued, 'he had been killed. There were five killed, among whom were the Secretaries of the Navy and State. I fainted and did not revive until someone was carrying me off the boat and I struggled so that I almost knocked us both off the gangplank. I did not know at the time, but I learned later it was the President whose life I almost consigned to the water. All five who were killed were buried from the White House in the Congressional cemetery. I remained at the White House until after the funeral and then I returned to our home, No. 43 Lafayette Place, New York. The President and I corresponded then and he paid me many nice little attentions. After I lost my father I felt differently toward the President. He seemed to fill the place and to be more agreeable in every way than any young man ever was or ever could be. He composed a very pretty song about me then—'Sweet Lady Awake.' At last he proposed again, and I wrote him I was willing this time, if my Mother would consent."

On April 20, 1844, Tyler wrote to Julia's mother, asking her consent to marry Julia:

"I have the permission of your dear daughter, Miss Julia Gardiner, to ask your approbation of my addresses to her, dear Madam, and to obtain your consent to our marriage which in all dutiful obedience she refers to your decision.

"May I indulge the hope that you will see in this nothing to object and that you will confer upon me the high privilege of substituting yourself in all that care and attention which you have so affectionately bestowed upon her. My position in society will I trust serve as a guarantee for the assurance which I give, that it will be the study of my life to advance her happiness by all and every means in my power.

"I pray you Madam to be assured of my highest regard and esteem.

John Tyler"

Mrs. Gardiner did not give her consent to the first letter, but after a second appeal by Tyler, she said she would not object to the marriage. Plans for a secret wedding were soon under way.

On June 26, 1844, President Tyler and Julia were married at the Church of the Ascension on Fifth Avenue in New York by Episcopal Bishop Benjamin Threadwell Onderdonk, assisted by the Rev. Dr. Bedell, the rector of the church. Only the bride's immediate family, the President's son and a few close friends were witnesses as the family was still in mourning for her father's death.

Julia wore a gown of white chiffon with a gauze veil falling from a circlet of white flowers wreathed in her hair.

The sight of the President and Julia leaving the church in an open barouche drawn by four white horses was the public's first inkling of the marriage.

The President, accompanied by his son, John Tyler, Jr., two or three Naval officers and Robert Rantoul of Boston, had left Washington the day before at six o'clock in the morning and arrived in New York that night at half past ten. They went directly to Howard's Hotel where the proprietor was sworn to secrecy as to their presence and the servants locked up to keep them from telling about the distinguished guest.

After the ceremony the next day, the wedding party breakfasted at the Gardiner residence on Lafayette Place, and then because the day was so hot, boarded the pleasure boat *Essex* for a cruise around New York Harbor.

A band was aboard and as the *Essex* passed through the harbor it received Presidential salutes from other ships in the harbor. At Jersey City, the President, his bride, his son, Julia's sister and three servants debarked and boarded a train for Philadelphia, where they were to spend the night.

At eleven o'clock they arrived at Hartwell's Hotel in Philadelphia, described as the "most excellent and favorite" in the city, where they were shown to the elegant suite of rooms usually occupied by Daniel Webster when he was in that city.

After being joined by Robert Tyler and his wife, Priscilla, the party sat down to an elegantly prepared supper consisting of cold woodcock, pigeons, chicken salad, oysters prepared in various ways and many other delicacies but no wines or liquors. These were strictly forbidden by the President and his bride.

The next morning the President was in high glee when the same small group sat down to a six o'clock breakfast in Black Dan's parlor, one of the hotel's finest public rooms. The menu included "Omelettes, spring chicken, ham and eggs, lamb chops, beef steaks, kidneys, pigeons, woodcock, salmon, veal cutlets, boiled eggs and young ducks."

While diving into a choice part of a young duck, the President remembered his unfinished business in Washington: winning Senate ratification of a treaty annexing Texas. He turned to his wife and said, "Well dear, we've ratified one treaty of immediate annexation, at least, without the advice and consent of the Senate." This brought laughs all around the table.

Immediately after breakfast they left for Washington by train, stopping at Baltimore, where crowds cheered them. The following day, the Tylers held a wedding reception in the flower-filled White House.

Throngs attended. John C. Calhoun, Tyler's new Secretary of State since the *Princeton* catastrophe, led the bride to a table in the center of the Blue Room and helped her cut the cake.

Julia wrote her mother that the reception was "very brilliant —brilliant to my heart's content," and added: "I have commenced my auspicious reign and am in quiet possession of the Presidential mansion."

A few days later, the honeymoon resumed as the newlyweds left Washington by boat for Old Point Comfort, in Virginia, where a new four-room cottage awaited them. The next two days were a ceaseless round of social activities, with all the officers at nearby Fort Monroe paying their respects.

From Old Point Comfort the couple went on to Sherwood Forest, the James River estate the President had bought as an investment shortly after his first wife's death. Before returning to Washington they spent part of their honeymoon at White Sulphur Springs, West Virginia, in a cottage that stands today on the spacious grounds of The Greenbrier Hotel, still a favorite spot for honeymooners.

Julia's happiness was reflected in her frequent and lengthy letters to her mother and sister. (Many of the letters are now in the library at Yale University.) Margaret accused Julia of spending "so much time in kissing, things of more importance are left undone," and her mother cautioned Julia to let her husband work during business hours.

"Business should take the precedence of caressing—reserve your caressing for private leisure and be sure you let no one see it unless you wish to be laughed at," she wrote.

Tyler, too, was supremely happy, and poetry in praise of his bride flowed from his lips and pen. If they ever worried about the 30 years difference in their ages, they gave no indication of it. On his 62nd birthday, 32-year-old Julia penned a poem to him on the subject. She said:

"Let ruthless age, then mark thy brow . . .

It need not touch thy heart . . .

And what e'er changes time may bring,

I'll love thee as thou art!"

Only eight months remained of Tyler's term when their honeymoon ended and the couple returned to Washington. There Julia reigned as First Lady in an establishment resembling court life.

At receptions she received in the Blue Room seated in a large armchair on a slightly raised platform surrounded by 12 maids of honor all dressed alike. Her headdress of bugles resembled a crown.

The mansion had not been so gay since Dolley Madison moved out. Julia initiated the tradition of having the Marine Band play "Hail to the Chief" whenever the President made an appearance, and won his approval of the quadrille, the polka and the waltz, that "vulgar" dance he had warned his daughters against years earlier.

During her time in the White House she wore black in the daytime and white or black lace over white in the evening. Before her father's death she always wore a diamond star on her forehead with a slender gold chain encircling her head. After his death she substituted a black stone for the diamond in her "Feronia," as it was called.

It was Julia Tyler who suggested that First Ladies' portraits be hung in the White House and hers shows her wearing a "Feronia."

Julia enjoyed being "Mrs. Presidentress." On December 6, 1844, she wrote a letter to her mother telling about her life as First Lady. She said:

"Last evening I had a most brilliant reception. The British Minister, Pakenham, was there with his secretary, and devoted to me. At least 50 members of Congress paid their respects to me, and all at one time. I did not enter the room until they had assembled. It really presented an array, and it was imposing to see them all brought forward and introduced one by one."

One of Tyler's goals during his administration was the annexation of Texas through a treaty requiring a ratification by two-thirds of the votes in the Senate. This became a bitter battle waged by Whigs and others who opposed the addition of any territory permitting slavery. Finally, Tyler won and Texas was admitted the month before his term ended.

Julia gave a grand ball to celebrate the victory and wore around her neck the "immortal gold pen" Tyler had used to sign the necessary annexation papers. She kept it as a treasure for many years but eventually it was lost.

Shortly before leaving the White House, Julia imported beautiful French mirrors, new rugs, chandeliers and other furniture from New York to furnish Sherwood Forest, the James River plantation house to which they retired upon leaving the Executive Mansion. Said to be the longest house in America at the time, it stretched out to a length of three hundred feet, with the main part of the white clapboard house two and a half stories high.

Here Julia happily reigned with splendor almost equal to that she had known in the White House. When visiting around the area, she rode in a fine carriage attended by coachmen and footmen in livery. For visits on the other side of the James River, she and the former President used a bright blue row boat named the *Pocahontas*, manned by four Negro oarsmen in livery. Their costumes were designed by Julia and consisted of bright blue and white checked calico shirts, white linen pants, black patent leather belts, straw hats painted blue with "Pocahontas" upon them in white, and in one corner of the shirt collar was a bow and arrow to signify Sherwood Forest and in the other the combined initials of Julia and her husband.

Tyler had not been a popular President despite his brilliant mind and literary talents, and he chose not to see another term in the office. When he left the White House in March 1845, though, the people "were happy, prosperous and contented," one writer of the day said. And in assessing Tyler's achievements, he cited that "he led the way and consummated the annexation of Texas, he settled the long mooted north eastern boundary question and defined the northern limit between this country and England; he saved the nation from the curse of National Bank," which had been the object of Henry Clay.

Tyler's popularity grew after he left office and he was in great demand as a speaker on questions of the day all around the country. These speeches took him often from his family at Sherwood Forest.

Notwithstanding the gossip provoked by the romance and secret marriage of Julia Gardiner and John Tyler, theirs was a happy union that lasted for 18 years. Julia bore Tyler seven children (he had eight by his first wife), making him the most prolific President.

His youngest child, Pearl, was born in 1861 when he was 70. The following January he died in Richmond, where he was serving in the Confederate Congress.

Julia suffered many financial losses during the Civil War. Sherwood Forest was stripped, and she went first to Richmond to live, then to her daughter's place on Staten Island. But after the death of her daughter Julia at the age of 21, she returned to Washington, where she found consolation in her conversion to Catholicism.

Julia petitioned Congress for a pension as a President's widow and received $3,000 annually. The pension was increased later to $5,000. Still regarded as a beauty in her fifties, she was swept up in the Capital's social whirl and was a guest at the White House during the Grant Administration.

Later she returned to Sherwood Forest, but she spent her last winter in Washington, where she presented her granddaughter to society. It was in Richmond, where she had gone after seeing her son Lyon installed as president of William and Mary College, that she spent her last days. There she died in 1889 at the age of 69. Death came to her in a hotel room directly across the hall from the room in which her husband had died nearly three decades earlier.

Julia and John Tyler's seven children were David Gardiner, who married Mary Mims Jones and became a member of Congress; John Alexander, who married Sarah Gardiner; Julia, who married William H. Spencer; Lachlan, who married Georgia Powell; Lyon, who married Annie Baker Tucker; Robert Fitzwalter, who married Fannie Glenn; and Pearl, who married William M. Ellis.

Only four of the children were living at the time of Julia's death.

Quotations from Tyler letters are by permission of Yale University Library.

President John Tyler and his bride, Julia Gardiner, spent part of their honeymoon in this cottage at White Sulphur Springs, West Virginia, on the grounds of the present Greenbrier Hotel. It is named The President's Cottage because so many Chiefs of State have made it their summer White House. Among those who stayed there in addition to Tyler were Van Buren, Fillmore, Pierce and Buchanan. The cottage was restored in 1957 as a museum.

Courtesy of The Greenbrier, White Sulpher Springs, W. Va.

NEWSPAPER

Entered according to the Act of Congress, in the year 1874, by FRANK LESLIE, in the office of the Librarian of Congress, at Washington.

XVIII]

NEW YORK, JUNE 6, 1874.

[PRICE, 10 CENTS,

THE WEDDING AT THE WHITE HOUSE

CEREMONY IN THE EAST ROOM—REV. DR. TIFFANY DECLARING MR. A. C. F. SARTORIS AND MISS NELLIE GRANT HUSBAND AND WIFE
SKETCHED BY OUR SPECIAL ARTIST, MR. HARRY OGDEN.

IX

Nellie Grant's Wedding

Nellie Grant - Algernon Charles Frederick Sartoris
May 21, 1874

he most brilliant White House wedding of the nineteenth century was that of Nellie Grant, only daughter of President Ulysses S. Grant, to Algernon Charles Frederick Sartoris, an Englishman. It also presented the spectacle of the saddest father ever to give away a bride in the Executive Mansion.

The stern President had made it plain that he would prefer that his daughter be an old maid. But if she must marry, he said, she should choose an American husband. Thus, as he led his daughter into the East Room on May 21, 1874, and placed her hand in that of the 23-year-old Sartoris, Grant made no effort to conceal his emotions or the tears in his eyes.

Sartoris had met Nellie aboard ship during a transatlantic crossing. The ensuing course of young love was a lot rougher than their ocean voyage.

When Sartoris first walked into the President's study at the White House and announced, "I want to marry your daughter," Grant's answer was no. He argued that Nellie, then 17, was too young to marry. Besides, a marriage to Sartoris would take her to another country to live.

The Englishman refused to give up, and Nellie added her pleadings to those of her suitor. It took them 18 months to wear down the President and obtain his reluctant consent, but once they did, Grant went all out to produce the outstanding social event of an eight-year administration that was notable for ostentatious entertaining.

President and Mrs. Grant sent wedding invitations to 200 persons, including the highest-ranking officials in government and close family friends, many of whom were famous as warriors, statesmen and millionaires. The invitation did not mention

The Rev. O. H. Tiffany pronounces Algernon Sartoris and Nellie Grant husband and wife in this sketch of the East Room ceremony by Harry Ogden, which appeared on the front page of Frank Leslie's Illustrated Newspaper June 6, 1874.

the names of either the bride or bridegroom. It said:

"The President and Mrs. Grant request the pleasure of your company at the marriage of their daughter, at the Executive Mansion on Thursday, May 21st, at eleven o'clock a.m."

Brown-eyed Nellie selected her trousseau in New York because there was not time to order it from Paris. It included three Indian shawls, a sacque of black Brussels lace, parasols with ivory handles, silk dresses of her favorite blue, yellow and rose, muslin dresses with French-worked flounces, gauzes, grenadines and hats for every occasion, slippers for each dress and delicately embroidered lingerie.

On her wedding day, a glorious spring morning with the fragrance of magnolia and catalpa heavy on the air, the Capital was buzzing with excitement. Police were stationed at all entrances to the White House grounds to admit only the 200 invited guests. The Grants had earlier had a fence built around the grounds, but Executive Avenue was thronged with people eager to get a glimpse of the guests arriving in 70 carriages.

Because the shutters were drawn over the windows of the East Room, the crowd missed more than it realized. In the first place, that chamber had been the triumph of the extensive redecorating ordered by Mrs. Grant shortly after she moved into the White House.

She had given it the full neo-Greek treatment, with tall pillars jutting from the frescoed walls and ornate false beams that split the ceiling into three sections. Each section was dominated by a colossal $1,800 chandelier made up of thousands of pieces of cut glass.

For Nellie's wedding day, the decorators added to all of this thousands of blossoms of tuberoses, spirea, lilies-of-the-valley and other fragrant flowers that filled the air with perfume. A dais at one side of the room was lavishly bowered with plants and evergreens. A rug given by the Sultan of Turkey covered the dais and over it was a floral arch supporting a large bell composed of snow-white blossoms.

Hanging from the ceiling just behind the marriage bell was a horizontal band of flowers. Near either end of it was a small floral circle, one bearing the bride's initials and the other the bridegroom's. White satin ribbons formed an aisle to this altar and guests were grouped behind the ribbons.

President Ulysses S. Grant who wept when he led his only daughter to the White House altar to marry an Englishman. From a portrait that hangs in the White House.

A few minutes before eleven, Mrs. Grant arrived with her sons, Ulysses and Jesse. Still in mourning for the death of her father, who had lived with them in the White House, she wore a black silk dress with lavender ribbons and flowers of lilacs and large pansies. Her dark hair fell in a ringlet down her back.

As the 40-piece Marine Band began to play the wedding march in the outer hall, the bridal party descended a private stairway. The bridegroom broke all precedents by carrying a bouquet of his own: orange blossoms and tuberoses with a center of pink buds from which a tiny flagstaff protruded. Its silver banner bore the word "Love."

He looked older than his 23 .years with his brown hair parted in the middle, his gray eyes, brown mustache and short side whiskers. He and his best man, Colonel Fred Grant, the bride's brother, walked slowly to the platform where the Rev. O. H. Tiffany, of the Metropolitan Methodist Episcopal Church, waited.

Next came the eight bridesmaids, daughters of the President's friends: Edith Fish, Bessie Conkling, Sallie Frelinghuysen, Lillie Porter, Jennie Sherman, Anna Barnes, Fannie Drexel, and Maggie Dent. They wore identical white corded silk with overdresses of white illusion and wide white sashes. Four carried blue bouquets and four carried pink ones.

The first two bridesmaids paused in the center of the room; the next two advanced beyond them, two more passing the last two, and Miss Barnes and Miss Fish stood at the foot of the dais.

Both the bride and her father were pale and the President looked unhappy. Brown-haired Nellie wore a $5,000 white satin dress of the richest material obtainable in New York. It was styled with wavy horizontal lines of delicate round point lace that ran across the front of the skirt and were intertwined with white flowers, green leaves and miniature oranges about the size of acorns. Two rows of the adorned lace trimmed the back of the skirt, sweeping to the right and the left towards the bottom. Beneath this were wide box pleats a considerable distance apart. The sleeves were long and expanded at the wrist.

Her bridal wreath was of white flowers and green leaves arranged with orange blossoms from which flowed a white tulle gossamer veil that enveloped the bride and extended to the floor. She wore high satin shoes bearing water stripes from the toes upwards. Her bouquet was of choice white flowers and she carried a pearl fan with lace cover.

The ceremony was brief and the voices low as the vows were exchanged. Secretary of State Hamilton Fish and Sir Edward Thornton, the British Ambassador, signed the marriage certificate, using pens on a small table covered with white silk in the center of the room. Then the guests went to the second-floor oval library where the wedding gifts, valued at $75,000, were displayed.

A. J. Drexel gave a dinner service valued at $4,500; George W. Childs, a dessert set of 84 pieces; Hamilton Fish, a silver tankard; General Orville Babcock, the President's secretary, a lace fan; and A. T. Stewart, a $500 handkerchief. There were innumerable silver punch bowls, ladles, saltcellars, spoons, glove boxes of fine gilt and carved wood, gold necklaces, lockets and bracelets.

The President and First Lady gave Nellie a necklace and earrings of diamonds, a pointlace fan, a bouquet, a lace handkerchief and a check for $10,000. But the most priceless gift was a poem by Walt Whitman, "A Kiss to the Bride." It closed:

"O youth and health! O sweet Missouri Rose! O bonnie bride! Yield thy red cheeks today unto a Nation's loving kiss."

State dinners during the Grant Administration were elaborate affairs lasting up to three hours and consisting of 29 courses with a break after the entree for Roman punch to fortify the guests, but the wedding breakfast in the State Dining Room was hard to excel in richness and flamboyance. From the pearly white bride's cake crowned with delicate flowers, in the center of the table, a floral ribbon extended to each end of the table. On these, and on trays of flowers at each end of the table, were tiny American flags wishing "Success to the President," "Success to the Supreme Court," "Success to the Army," "Hail Columbia." Around these were pyramids of nougat candy and around the edge of the table was a delicate line of flowers.

At each place was a menu printed on white satin and tied with white ribbon. Listed on it were:

Soft crabs on toast. Gateaux garnis de Crabes and Champignons, Sauce a la Creme. Croquettes of Chicken

with Green Peas, Cotelettes d'agneaut, Sauce a la Tar-
tare, Aspic de langues de boeuf a la Moderne. Wood
cocks and snipes on toast, decorated. Broiled spring
chickens. Salade Sauce, Maillonaise. Strawberries with
cream. Bride cake—center piece. Side piece of Charlotte
Russes and Croque en bouche. Corbeils glaces a la
Jardiniere. Gateaux de trois freres. Epigraphe la fleur,
de Nelly Grant. Pudding a la Nesselerode Sauce a la
Creme. Corbeils d'Oranges garnis de fraises. Gelee,
Blamangee a la Napoleon. Plombieres garnies de fruits
a fleures glaces. Ice cream of various flavors. Water ices
of various flavors. Small fancy cakes. Punch a la Ro-
maine. Coffee. Chocolate.

For each guest to carry home and dream on there was a
slice of wedding cake in a little box tied with white silk.

At twelve o'clock the bride went upstairs to change into her
travel costume—a blue redingote and jauntily tilted blue felt
hat. At fifteen minutes after one she and her husband emerged
from the front door and with the bride's youngest brother,
Ulysses, were driven in the President's four-in-hand team to the
Baltimore and Potomac depot.

A special Pullman palace car made for the Vienna Exposi-
tion and decorated for this occasion with American and English
flags, flowers and evergreens took them to New York. They
sailed the following day for England.

During their drive to the depot, the chimes of the Metro-
politan Methodist Church rang out with Mendelssohn's Wed-
ding March, "The Wedding Pearl," "Hail Columbia," "God
Save the Queen," "Then You'll Remember Me," "Auld Lang
Syne," the Grand March from "Tannhauser," and "Home
Sweet Home."

After the couple left the White House, the President was
found in Nellie's room sobbing unrestrainedly. The following
day, he and Mrs. Grant met their daughter and son-in-law at
the Fifth Avenue Hotel in New York and later saw them off on
the *Baltic* to a new life in England.

The wedding was a brilliant climax to Nellie's gay charming life as the belle in the White House. She had been a promising beauty of 14 when the Grants moved into the Executive
Mansion and the apple of her father's eye. When she went

away to finishing school, for instance, the President escorted her personally to Miss Porter's in Connecticut because, he said, "Mrs. Grant would only cry and bring her back." But on his way back to the White House, he found three telegrams from Nellie awaiting him in New York. They all said, "I am about to die from homesickness." He wired her to come home, and sent an escort for her.

In the White House, Nellie assisted her mother in entertaining. And entertaining reached a new peak after the dreary war years. Grant was a popular President, having been elected by an overwhelming majority because of his magnificent record during the Civil War. Mrs. Grant held weekly receptions, calling on Cabinet wives and other friends to assist her. These ladies were always invited to lunch in the family dining room beforehand.

Then there were the traditional open houses on New Year's and the Fourth of July; everyone was invited, chambermaids and countesses, laborers and lawmakers.

Once a week the Grants gave a dinner, usually for 36 persons, and these sometimes cost as much as $2,000. The State Dining Room was garlanded with roses and evergreens with elaborate table decorations including epergnes of fruit and masses of flowers. The center piece often was a solid silver ship with a figure depicting Hiawatha sailing on a mirrored lake. This had been given to the White House by the Mohawk Indians.

The food was as famous as the decorations at these events for Mrs. Grant had replaced the quartermaster installed in the kitchen by the President with an Italian steward named Melah, who had worked at some of the most fashionable hotels in the country.

The elegant dinners he prepared and served were described by Emily Edson Briggs, a newspaper correspondent who left a record of social Washington during the Reconstruction period, in her book, *The Olivia Letters*, as follows:

"In the beginning of the feast, fruit, flowers, and sweetmeats grace the table, whilst bread and butter give only a Spartan simplicity to the 'first course,' which is composed of a French vegetable soup, and according to the description by those who have tasted it, no soup, foreign or domestic, has ever been known to equal it.

"The ambrosial soup is followed by a French croquet of meat. Four admirably trained servants remove the plates between each course, and their motions are as perfect as clockwork. These servants are clad in garments of faultless cut, which serve to heighten to the last degree their sable complexion. White kid gloves add the finishing touch to this part of the entertainment. The third 'course' of the dinner is composed of a fillet of beef, flanked on each side by potatoes the size of a walnut, with plenty of mushrooms to keep them company. The next course is dainty in the extreme. It is made up entirely of luscious leg of partridges, and baptized by a French name entirely beyond my comprehension. It will readily be seen that a full description of the twenty-nine courses would be altogether too much for the healthy columns of a newspaper to bear, so we pass to the dessert, not omitting to say that the meridian or noon of the feast is marked by the guests being served bountifully with frozen punch. As a general rule, wine is served about every third course. Six wineglasses of different sizes and a small bouquet of flowers are placed before each guest at the beginning.

"The dessert is inaugurated by the destruction of a rice pudding, it is such a pudding as would make our grandmothers clap their hands with joy. After the rice pudding, canned peaches, pears and quinces are served. Then follow confectionery, nuts, ice-cream, coffee, and chocolate, and with these warm, soothing drinks, the Presidential entertainment comes to an end, and the host and his guests repair to the Red Room, and after fifteen minutes spent in conversation the actors in a state dinner rapidly disappear."

In between assisting her mother in her social functions, Nellie herself was entertaining her own young friends and being entertained by them. Her presence was sought at gatherings throughout the city. Newspapers gave glowing accounts of her activities. One said "she was almost daily seen on the prominent thoroughfares in a light phaeton behind a span of black ponies, usually accompanied by her most intimate friend, Miss Anna Barnes, daughter of the Surgeon General of the Army."

Nellie loved to dance, but the First Lady would not permit her to attend parties without one of her brothers as an escort. Usually it was Jesse, three years her junior, and he was generally bored by the parties he had to attend with her. Once he took her to a Navy dance at Annapolis and forgot to remove her galoshes before she went merrily whirling on the floor.

There was beginning to be talk about Nellie's many suitors and the late hours she kept. When she was 16, she was sent abroad partly because Mrs. Grant thought travel might broaden her education and partly to remove the hazard of romantic entanglements and possibly an early marriage.

Travelling under the chaperonage of the former Secretary of the Navy and Mrs. Adolph E. Borie, who had long been family friends of the Grants, Nellie was received by Queen Victoria at Buckingham Palace and given a great whirl by Robert C. Shenck, U.S. Minister to England, and Adam Badeau, U.S. Consul General in England.

Returning home abroad the steamship *Russia*, she met Algernon Sartoris, a dashing Oxford-educated Englishman whose father had been a member of Parliament and whose mother was a sister of the famous actress Fanny Kemble. He was handsome and rich, with a pleasing personality and a musical voice for singing.

The young couple fell in love on shipboard, but when they reached Washington, they discovered that her parents objected to the match and even his parents were not optimistic about their marital prospects. The latter wrote apologetically to President Grant about Algy. One of his problems was drinking.

The match was also opposed by many of the Grants' intimate friends and by masses of Americans who regarded Nellie as the pet of the Nation and considered any Englishman unworthy of her hand.

It was not surprising, then, that hardly before the wedding music had faded, it was widely predicted that Nellie would soon be suing for divorce. But friends who visited her in England found her very much in love with Algy and contented with the English country life that his income of $60,000 a year permitted them to enjoy.

Two years later, Nellie returned to the White House for a visit, bringing her first baby, Algernon Edward. The Sartorises later had two daughters, Vivian May and Rosemary Alice. They brought their children to America nearly every year to visit her parents.

President Grant eventually became reconciled to the marriage and presented his son-in-law with a trotting horse and American buggy.

Nevertheless, there were rumors that all was not well with the marriage, and by 1889, Nellie was ready to admit that the match was a failure. She returned to the United States with her children and with her widowed mother took a house in Washington. All doors were open to her from the start, and she was frequently a guest at White House functions.

Sartoris went to Italy, where he died four years after their separation.

Years later Nellie married Frank J. Jones of Chicago, an Assistant Postmaster General in the Cleveland Administration, in a ceremony in Canada.

This picture of Nellie Grant and Algernon Sartoris in a framed setting of cupids and flowers was published in The New York Daily Graphic, May 24, 1874.

X

Another Grant Wedding

Ida Marie Honoré - Frederick Dent Grant
October 20, 1874

he same year that Nellie Grant married her Englishman in a brilliant White House wedding, her elder brother, Frederick Dent Grant, was married in what a newspaper of that day described as "one of the most brilliant weddings ever witnessed in the West."

The ceremony was held on October 20, 1874, in Chicago at the summer residence of the bride's parents, Mr. and Mrs. Henry Hamilton Honoré.

Newspaper correspondents from all over the country gathered in Chicago two weeks before the day, waiting for the event that would unite in holy matrimony the beautiful 20-year-old Ida Marie Honoré and the son of the President and Mrs. Ulysses S. Grant.

Four years earlier the Honorés' older daughter, Bertha, had married wealthy Potter Palmer in another ceremony that had kept Chicago talking for months, and this one promised to be just as exciting.

For days before the Grant-Honoré nuptials, members of the Honoré and Palmer families had to relinquish almost all other business to lend a hand to the wedding plans. They were besieged by reporters, who interviewed everyone from housemaids to dry-goods clerks for details about the wedding gown, decorations and nuptial plans.

Colonel Grant, a graduate of West Point, was serving in Chicago on the staff of General Sheridan, a close friend of the

Ida Marie Honoré who married Fred Grant, son of President and Mrs. Ulysses S. Grant, in a brilliant wedding in Chicago in October, 1874. The diamond cross she wears was a wedding gift.

President, when he met Marie Honoré at a dinner party given by her sister, Mrs. Potter Palmer.

This was eight months before the wedding. The small group at that dinner included Miss Irene Rucker and her sister, Miss Mary Hall, General Phil Sheridan, General Forsyth, and Adrian Honoré, brother of the hostess.

It was a case of love at first sight for both Fred and Marie and after a few weeks of courtship, Grant proposed and was accepted. Wedding plans were begun immediately.

Grant was 25 at the time and very handsome in his well-cut Army uniform. He had a soldierly build, very much the counterpart of his father, was of medium height with brown hair and a light mustache that gave him added dash.

Marie was a lovely brunette with dark brown eyes and a peaches-and-cream complexion. She was smaller than average in height and had a fine figure. She had graduated with honors three years earlier at the Convent of the Visitation in Washington, D.C., and had taken an extra year there to continue her musical studies. She had a fine mezzo-soprano voice and played both the piano and the harp.

Her great grandfather, John A. Honoré, had come from Paris in 1808 at the age of 30 and settled in Louisville, Kentucky. He had three children—two girls and a boy. The latter, Francis, entered the wholesale business with his father and helped to increase the family's wealth. One of his three sons, Henry Hamilton, married Eliza Carr, a daughter of Captain John Carr, one of the pioneers in Oldham County, Kentucky. Marie was one of Henry and Eliza's six children. The family moved to Chicago when Marie was two years old.

Their town mansion on Michigan Avenue, opposite what is now the Chicago Museum, had burned in a ravaging fire that swept the city and at the time Marie married, the family was living in their summer residence, facing Vincennes Avenue between 46th and 47th Streets.

It was in this lovely setting, half rural, half town that the wedding was held. The house was a two-story and basement frame structure surrounded by ten acres and bounded by Grand Boulevard in the rear.

President and Mrs. Grant traveled to Chicago for the wedding and arrived at the house just in time for the three o'clock ceremony. They were much happier on this occasion than they had been at Nellie's wedding for they approved of Fred's choice. As the wedding guests came, to the strains of music by Johnny Hand's Orchestra, one of the Midwest's finest, lines of spectators encircled the spacious grounds and the band of the Grand Western Light Guard presented their own free concert in front of the house.

The bridegroom thrilled the spectators by driving up to the house in an open wagon drawn by four well-curried army mules with jingling harness and burnished hooves.

This was an era of opulence and elegance and the house was decorated accordingly. Walls of the front parlor were covered with green vines studded at intervals with bunches of roses, camellias, carnations, pinks, bouvardies, heliotrope and Spanish jasmine.

The chandelier was entwined with garlands of buds and leaves and from the center hung a huge basket of moss roses, tuberoses and lily of the valley. From each corner of the room extending to the chandelier were festoons of smilax and maurondias, giving the impression of a fairy bower. In the fireplace was a bank of flowers and on the mantel were two tall gilded vases of feathery ferns rising almost to the ceiling. From the edge of the mantel and over the bank of flowers in the fireplace was suspended a floral monogram of English violets and red and white buds forming the letters "H" and "G."

Two white columns between the front and back parlors were entwined with smilax and ivy. The back parlor, where the ceremony was held, was more elaborately decorated than the front one. The mantel was almost hidden with a profusion of white flowers. An arched recess at the back of the room was draped in deep red rep, forming a background for three Carrara marble statues: Miss Hosmer's "Puck," Rosetti's "Veiled Cupid," and Randolph Rogers' "Nydia, the Blind Girl of Pompeii."

Over the recess were trailing vines and flowers and in the center was the shield of the United States. The stripes in the shield were formed by red, white and blue bouvardies, and the ground for the stars by English violets. Each star was formed by a single bouvardie. The initials "H" and "G" in flowers hung above the shield.

The dais upon which the bridal couple stood for the exchange of vows was beneath a floral canopy with a green moss background with alternate stripes of pinks and heliotrope. Fragrant pink and mauve Roman hyacinths stood on small stands at each corner of the room.

At ten minutes past three, as the orchestra played Mendelssohn's Wedding March, the bridal procession, formed in an upstairs room, entered the parlor. First came General Forsyth and Miss Dunlevy; next Lieutenant Larned and Irene Rucker, then Adrian Honoré and a Miss Houston of Kentucky, and finally, U. S. Grant, Jr., brother of the bridegroom, and Mary Hall, cousin of the bride.

Behind them came the bride, on the arm of her father, and the bridegroom, in full dress uniform, escorting the mother of the bride. As the bridal couple took their place beneath the canopy, her parents stood behind them, President and Mrs. Grant were at their left, and Mr. and Mrs. Potter Palmer were at the right.

The Rev. Isaac Erritt, pastor of the Christian Church of Chicago, of which the bride's father was a member, performed the ceremony. At the end, before Fred had a chance to kiss his bride, she was engulfed with embraces and kisses from others, first her mother, then her sister, then Mrs. Grant and the President.

The bride wore a Paris gown of white satin with an overdress of imported Brussels lace, a gift from her sister, Mrs. Palmer. Her satin corsage was stiffened with a hundred boned stays and trimmed with lace of the same design as the overskirt. The sleeves were in the Duchess style. Her veil was of snowy tulle, full and reaching to the hem of the satin skirt. It was fastened to the left side of her head by a bunch of orange blossoms from which a trailing wreath of three flounces hung to the bottom of the veil.

She wore a pearl necklace, a gift from President and Mrs. Grant, bracelets given by her aunt, Mrs. Benjamin Honoré, and a $10,000 set of diamond solitaire earrings and cross, which were a gift from her brother-in-law, Potter Palmer.

Next to the bride's gown, the most elegant dress in the room was that worn by Mrs. Palmer. It was silver-colored satin trimmed with ruffled flounces lined with cardinal red silk.

Colonel Frederick D. Grant, eldest son of President and Mrs. Ulysses S. Grant, who brought his bride to live in the White House.

After the ceremony the guests went into the dining room, where the 14-foot table was laid with a service of French-cut glass and fine silver. In the center was a silver bowl of flowers measuring two and one-half feet in diameter, and roses of all colors and feathery vines were draped over and down the sides of the table. Molded ice cream in various designs were at the four corners of the table, and on each side were two tall forms of boned game in jelly.

The menu was printed on tinted paper in delicate letters of mauve. One side read:

*Wedding Collation
in honor of
Colonel and Mrs. Frederick Dent Grant
at the residence of
Mr. and Mrs. H. H. Honoré
Vincennes Avenue and Forty-seventh Street
Chicago
October 20, 1874*

On the other side was the menu:

Stewed Terrapin, Escalloped Oysters

Patties of Sweetbreads, Patties of Turkey

Patties of Oysters, Chicken Salad, Lobster Salad

Fillets of Snipes in Paper cases

Boned Quail in jelly form

Boned Prairie Chicken in jelly form

Centerpiece—Natural Flowers

Groom's Cake decorated with natural flowers

Bride's Cake decorated with natural flowers

Assorted Cakes

Vanilla, Lemon, Strawberry,

Peach, Chocolate and Coffee Ice Cream

Charlotte Russe, Charlotte Glaces

Biscuit Glace, Peach Meringues

Strawberry Meringues, Apricot Meringues

Port Wine Jelly, Sherry Wine Jelly, Champagne Jelly

Grapes, Pears, Bananas, Oranges, Fruit Salad

Tea   Coffee   Krug   Private Cuvée   Frappé

Additional guests were invited to the reception, at which the orchestra, almost concealed in an enclosed veranda hung with crimson rep ornamented with ferns, played a program of music. Selections were:

Overture to "Zampa"—Herald.

Selections from "Trovatore"—Neuman.

Cornet Solo "How Fair Thy Art"—Gambert.

Waltz "Myrtle Bouquet"—Strauss.

Fantasia "Martha"—Strauss.

Fantasia "L'Eclair"—Haller.

Waltz "Tresche Geister"—Strauss.

Offenbachiana—Conradi.

Fantasia "Sweet Longings"—Menzel.

Concert Overture—Leutner.

Galop "Auf Reisen"—Conradi.

Gifts were displayed in an upstairs room. Among them was a large case of butter plates of solid silver lined with gold, half a dozen silver salt stands, a silver cup and saucer and spoon—all monogrammed and all the gift of Mr. and Mrs. A.

J. Drexel of Philadelphia, who had given Nellie Grant a $4,500 dinner service.

At nine o'clock that evening the bridal couple took the train to St. Louis, where they began their honeymoon. They went to central New York and visited West Point before returning to Washington, where they lived at the White House with President and Mrs. Grant.

Fred was away part of the time during the first two years of their marriage as his military assignments took him to various parts of the country. He was one of General Custer's officers during his battles with the Indians, and in June 1876, while Fred was on leave to be with his wife at the White House for the birth of their first child, Custer made his last stand and his men were massacred.

The baby, Julia, who was named for her grandmother, was christened in the East Room and was held by her nurse in the receiving line at the reception President and Mrs. Grant gave in the White House on New Year's Day 1877.

When she was 13, her father was appointed American Minister to Vienna. At 17, Julia was presented to the Austrian court, and when the family returned to the United States, she made her debut at parties given by her mother in New York, her grandmother in Washington, and her aunt in Chicago.

After the Cleveland Administration took office, Fred settled in New York, joining Theodore Roosevelt as a New York City Police Commissioner. Marie entertained at elegant dinner parties where the guests included such famous persons as Joseph Choate, William Evarts, Mark Hanna, Chauncey Depew and Elihu Root. Root's daughter later married Fred and Marie's son, U. S. Grant III.

When the Spanish-American war broke out, Fred went back into the Army and at the time of his death in 1912, he was a major general on active duty. Ida Marie returned to Washington to live until her death in 1930.

Julia married a Russian nobleman, Prince Cantacuzene, and lived in Russia for nearly 20 years until the revolution, when she and her husband fled. Now 90, she lives in Washington, D.C. Shortly before her 90th birthday she regained partial eyesight after ten years of total blindness. U. S. Grant III, a retired Army general, also lives in Washington.

XI

This Wedding
Sparkled Without
Champagne

Emily Platt - Russell Hastings
June 19, 1878

mily Platt, President Rutherford B. Hayes's 27-year-old niece, was married in the oval Blue Room of the White House to General Russell Hastings of Ohio on June 19, 1878.

Daughter of the President's late sister, Fanny, and William Augustus Platt of Columbus, Ohio, Emily had lived with the Hayes family most of the time since her mother died in 1856 when Emily was only 6 years old.

When she moved into the White House with the President and Mrs. Hayes, she was not only like a daughter to the family but was also an excellent executive, handling all the details of the First Lady's social calendar.

Her fiancé had been one of the first volunteers to enlist when the Civil War broke out, serving in the 23rd regiment, Ohio Volunteer Infantry, which was the regiment of two future Presidents: Hayes and William McKinley. During the battle of Opequan, Virginia, in 1864, Hastings was severely wounded in the knee, an injury that left the tall, erect figure lame for life.

He first met Emily during the war in Columbus where she was "scraping lint and rolling bandages," but it was not until years later, in 1877, when he called at the White House to renew his personal friendship with his former brigade commander who was now President that he met her again.

Hastings had been a widower for three years when the President's niece caught his eye. He noticed that she had a beautiful complexion, dark brown hair, a gentle manner and gift for conversation. She was also quick, well-educated and had traveled in foreign countries as well as her own.

Their friendship soon turned to romance and the wedding date was set for June 19. Both hoped to keep the wedding a small, quiet event but the President and First Lady wanted to

An artist's drawing of the marriage of Miss Emily Platt, niece of President Rutherford B. Hayes, to General Russell Hastings in the Blue Room of the White House on June 19, 1878. (From the New York Daily Graphic, June 25, 1878).

give their niece a beautiful wedding to remember. Though the guest list was limited, the White House was lavishly decorated for the occasion.

The Blue Room, then paneled in bright blue with gray between the panels, was banked with flowers—geraniums, fuschias and foliage plants.

In front of the windows hung a wedding bell of white roses with a rope of green festooned on each side. In each festoon was a hoop of white blossoms with the bride's initials, E. P., centering one and R. H., the bridegroom's initials, in the other. Wreaths of roses and pansies hung beneath the wall sidelights, and the chandeliers were festooned with smilax.

The corridors were decorated with potted palms, shrubs and cut flowers; many friends of the bride had sent floral souvenirs and these were incorporated in the wedding decorations.

At seven o'clock on the evening of the wedding, the scarlet-coated Marine Band in the hall struck up Mendelssohn's wedding march and the bridal party entered the Blue Room. First came the President and Laura Platt Mitchell, the bride's sister, who wore a gown of pale blue satin and damasse, its drapery caught by bunches of tea roses and decorated with bands embroidered in pale straw shade and fringed with blue.

General Russell Hastings

They were followed by the bridegroom and Mrs. Hayes, wearing an eggshell gown of soft silk designed in the princess style with a long train and a shawl-shaped drape of chenille damask gauze.

The bride entered on the arm of her father, who had remarried following her mother's death. Her elegant gown of ivory brocade was fashioned along princess lines with a long train bordered with deep pleating of plain silk, caught at the top with a wreath of orange blossoms. Wreaths of orange blossoms also trimmed each side of the gown, and down the front were bows of white double-faced ribbon.

The square neckline was filled with tulle, caught with a spray of orange blossoms, and single blossoms held puffs of illusion bordering the neck. Ruffles of plain silk edged the sleeves, which reached half way to the wrist.

The bride's dress was made especially for her in New York but was not considered elaborate by fashion standards of the day because there was no lace.

The tulle veil, which was held by a wreath of orange blossoms, was short and square in front, covering the face, and very long and full in back. It was caught below the waist on the skirt by another spray of orange blossoms, which were all of wax.

There were only six in the bridal procession for the couple had no attendants. The wedding was for the most part a family affair with many children present. The President's 11-year-old daughter Fannie wore a dress of white Victoria lawn, with ruffles and flounces of embroidery and sashed in colored ribbon. Also invited to witness the wedding was Winnie Monroe, the nurse who took care of the Hayes children.

Bishop Thomas A. Jagger came from the Southern diocese of Ohio to officiate and performed the Episcopal ceremony while the bridal couple stood beneath the marriage bell.

During the evening the Marine Band played a delightful serenade including selections from "Norma," the "Mande Waltz," "Robin Adair," "Pizzicato Polka," "Fantasia" from "Trovatore," "La Gavotte," Overture from "Fra Diavolo" and "Le Stregon Galop."

An elaborate supper was spread in the family dining room following the ceremony, and the elegant vermeil dessert service purchased by President Monroe in 1817 was brought out for the occasion.

At each end of the long table was a tall, snow white bride's cake decorated with the initials of the bride and bridegroom in blue. A bouquet was at each place, with baskets of fruit, pyramids of ices and flowers in flat dishes, and plates of bonbons on the table.

Toasts to the bride were given in tea, coffee and lemonade for there was no wine served at the wedding festivities. Both President and Mrs. Hayes were temperance leaders and they established a policy that no wines or liquors would be served in the White House. This policy won both praise and criticism and led to the nickname of "Lemonade Lucy" for the First Lady.

Most applause for the policy came from the Women's Christian Temperance Union, then headed by Frances Willard, which presented a life-size portrait of Lucy Hayes by Daniel Huntington to the White House for its collection. In it she wears a ruby red dress, with sleeves and filled-in neck, and stands holding a small cluster of roses.

Gifts for the bridal couple were numerous and costly and included an exquisite ormolu and silver clock, a tiny watch encrusted with diamonds, a triple necklace of pearls, a silver tea set, and a generous check from the President.

The bride slipped away from the wedding supper to change to her going-away outfit of a summer-weight camel's hair combined with silk of the same shade, which had also been made for her in New York.

The President's carriage whirled out of the White House drive with the newlyweds, taking them to the depot just in time for the train to New York. After a long summer at Cushing's Island in the harbor of Portland, Maine, the Hastings returned to the White House in October.

Emily took up her old duties but her husband was stranded with nothing to do. One morning over their breakfast table at the White House, they decided to pull up stakes in Washington and spend the winter in Bermuda. The General's old war wound caused him distress in winter and he had often journeyed to the warmer climates of Italy, Bermuda and New Orleans.

"With almost wilful obstinacy we struck for life and liberty, and during the first week of January, 1879, we steamed out of New York harbor on the little eight hundred ton steamship 'Canima,' bound for Bermuda Islands . . ." General Hastings later recorded.

In 1883, the General and Emily returned to the site of their second honeymoon, Bermuda, and built a home, "Soncy," on Point Share, Saltine Bay.

Three children were born to this marriage—Lucy Webb, Fanny and Russell Platt Hastings.

General Hastings died in 1904 and Emily died in 1922.

ARRIVAL OF MISS FOLSOM IN WASHINGTON.

MISS FOLSOM WELCOMED BY THE PRESIDENT.

PRESIDENT CLEVELAND'S MARRIAGE.

INCIDENTS OF THE SIMPLE BUT IMPRESSIVE CEREMONY AT THE WHITE HOUSE.

THE marriage of President Cleveland to Miss Frances Folsom, the announcement of which had raised such a universal and pleasing flutter of sentiment, took place exactly in accordance with the pre-arranged programme, at seven o'clock on Wednesday evening of last week. Not a mishap or a miscalculation marred the becomingly simple celebration of the event. The fair young bride came like a morning sunbeam into the stately mansion which she is to rule as first lady of the land. In the evening, amidst the traditional shower of rice and old slippers, she left it as the President's wife; and the newly married pair sped away to their honeymoon retreat in the Alleghany Mountains, followed by the hearty felicitations of fifty millions of good Americans, to say nothing of friends in other quarters of the globe.

The President's first meeting with his fiancée after her return from Europe took place in New York on Decoration Day, and by Tuesday morning he was back at his desk in Washington. Miss Folsom made the journey on Tuesday night. Attended by her mother and her cousin, Mr. Benjamin Folsom, she left New York via Jersey City in a special car attached to the 8:30 train on the Baltimore and Ohio Railroad. The curiosity of reporters, passengers and crowds of people along the route was successfully baffled, and when the train rolled into Washington at half-past five o'clock Wednesday morning, only a few spectators were on hand. Miss Rose Elizabeth Cleveland met the party at the station, and hurried them off in a carriage to the White House. The morning was a beautiful one, and the June sunshine showered its benison upon the pretty bride. The President, with extended hands, greeted her at the entrance to the corridor. There was a good deal of kissing amongst the bride's lady relatives, and possibly this affectionate mode of salutation was not altogether confined to the feminine side of the party.

The South Room, next to the library, on the second floor, which General Grant and Mrs. Grant used to occupy, had been set apart for the bride's use. It was beautifully decked with flowers, as were all the other principal apartments of the mansion. The East Room was festooned with roses, and adorned with floral shields in the national colors, the central feature being a semicircular mass of palms and ferns of graded sizes at the east side of the room. The Green Room also contained an abundance of palms, ferns, arbor vitæ, and cut flowers. The Blue Room, where the marriage ceremony was to be performed, had been so elaborately decorated that scarcely a trace of its nominal color was visible. The wall opposite the corridor was a symphony in green. On the hearth under the east mantel lay a mass of begonia rubra, whose scarlet blossoms were designed to represent a glowing fire. Centaureas scattered at the base were meant for ashes. Extending from these designs was a mosaic of blossoms, a lower plane, which carried out the idea of a tiled floor of the hearth. Vines ran from the hearth to the mantel, on which reposed a bed of dark pansies with the inscription, "June 1886," in light blossoms. The west mantel, really across the room, was built by the same idea from the bottom, in a design similar to the other. The mantel-top, however, presented a brighter sight with its solid bank of choice

DEPARTURE OF THE PRESIDENT AND HIS BRIDE FROM THE WHITE HOUSE—THE SHOWER OF RICE

MRS. OSCAR FOLSOM, MOTHER-IN-LAW OF PRESIDENT CLEVELAND.
PHOTO. BY McMICHAEL, OF BUFFALO.

XII

President Cleveland Takes a Bride

Frances Folsom - Grover Cleveland
June 2, 1886

f all the weddings in the White House, the most historic was that of Grover Cleveland and Frances Folsom. Never before had a President of the United States been married in the Executive Mansion and one has not been married there since.

The bachelor President Grover Cleveland was 49 when he married his 21-year-old ward.

The formal announcement of the wedding date was flashed from Washington only four days before the event, held at seven o'clock on the evening of June 2, 1886.

But theirs was no whirlwind romance or courtship. The President had known Frances from babyhood and had even helped select her first baby carriage. Her father, Oscar Folsom, was his first law partner in Buffalo, New York, and when Folsom was killed after being thrown from a carriage in 1875, he left Cleveland as guardian of his 11-year-old daughter.

Cleveland helped Mrs. Folsom and her young daughter in many ways and supervised the education of his ward with keen interest, watching her grow up into a beautiful young woman. Frances finished her courses at Central School in Buffalo, then entered Wells College to complete her formal education.

Her nickname, Frank, suited her open, winning personality. She was natural and unaffected but did everything with a vim and dash that left her distinctive mark wherever she went. She loved flowers and had a flair for amateur photography.

Just when Cleveland's paternal interest in his ward turned into courtship would be hard to say, but the letters and flowers from him became more and more frequent while she was in college. By the time Frances graduated from Wells in June 1885, the gossips were buzzing about an impending engagement between the President and Miss Folsom.

An artist's version of the departure of President Cleveland and his bride from the White House under a shower of rice. (From Frank Leslie's Illustrated Newspaper, June 12, 1886).

And they were right. Before Frances sailed off with her mother for a European tour—a graduation gift—members of the family were told of the secret engagement.

The wedding was to take place at the home of the bride's grandfather, Colonel John B. Folsom of Folsomdale, near Buffalo. But "Papa John," as Frances called her grandfather, died while mother and daughter were on their way home from Europe and the burden of changing wedding plans fell on the President himself.

He sent his secretary and confidant, Colonel Daniel Lamont, to meet Frances when the *Noordland* sailed into New York harbor with mother and daughter aboard. The efficient Lamont managed to evade eager newspaper reporters and whisked the Folsoms from the ship to Gilsey House without a hitch.

As personal intermediary for the President, the Colonel talked over the wedding plans with Frances, then left for Washington the same evening, with the following Wednesday, June 2, set for the wedding day.

That night the announcement was made at the White House and the next day the world knew the President would take a bride within the historic walls of the Executive Mansion.

President Cleveland himself wrote out the invitations to the family, Cabinet members and a few friends who would witness the event. The simple invitation read:

> Executive Mansion
> May 29, 1886
>
> My dear Mr. ————,
>
> I am to be married on Wednesday evening at seven o'clock at the White House to Miss Folsom. It will be a very quiet affair and I will be extremely gratified at your attendance on the occasion.
>
> Yours sincerely,
> Grover Cleveland

The unique invitations were sent to so few that today they are rare collectors' items. The White House is still seeking one of the historical mementoes for its own collection of wedding memorabilia.

Supervising every detail of the wedding, President Cleveland called in the White House head gardener Paster, to arrange a plan for decorating the Blue Room, and his instructions banned floral bells and horseshoes.

Several days before the wedding, John Philip Sousa, the director of the Marine Band, was asked to submit a program of wedding music. His list included Arditi's "I Am a Rose," and a number from his own opera, "Désirée," listed as a quartette, "The Student of Love." The President studied the program carefully.

"I think I'd play that number just as "A Quartette," leaving out 'The Student of Love'," the President advised the composer-conductor.

Then Sousa and Colonel Lamont carefully measured off the steps to the proposed Blue Room altar to correspond with the notes of Mendelssohn's wedding march.

On Sunday, Memorial Day, the President took an afternoon train for New York, where, at last, he had a rendezvous with his fiancée at Gilsey House.

Benjamin Folsom, the bride's cousin who had accompanied her and her mother on the European tour, was there to escort the President from the Jersey City depot to Gilsey House. He waited, unknown and unnoticed, until the President saw him in the crowd. As the President passed through the throng of well-wishers, one called out: "Good for you, Grover."

New Yorkers were delighted by the sight of the portly President as he reviewed two Decoration Day parades. A band lapsed into "He's Going to Marry Yum Yum."

Frances watched a parade from the Fifth Avenue Hotel and the busy President managed to dine with her in her parlor at Gilsey House. But there were memorial services at General Grant's tomb and at the Academy of Music that demanded the presence of the President before he returned at midnight to Washington.

There was a slight misty rain falling when the train bringing the bride arrived at the Baltimore and Potomac depot in Washington shortly after five-thirty on the morning of her wedding day.

Colonel Lamont was on hand to meet Frances, her mother, cousin Benjamin and a Mrs. Rogers of Syracuse. Numerous

Crowds gather outside the White House for a glimpse of the wedding inside of President Grover Cleveland and Frances Folsom. Drawn by Charles Graham for Harper's Weekly.

The President's Wedding, drawn by T. de Thulstrup for Harper's Weekly, June 12, 1886.

bundles, hat boxes, shawl straps and bits and pieces of luggage had to be collected before they stepped into the Presidential carriage, where Rose Cleveland, the President's sister, who had been his official White House hostess, was waiting to accompany the bride and her party for the drive to the White House.

The President, with outstretched hands, greeted his fiancée at the entrance of the corridor, and the servants were waiting to get a glimpse of the lovely girl who would soon be the mistress of the White House.

The President joined his guests for an eight o'clock breakfast, and took time from the affairs of state to sit down with Frances and take care of one last detail for their wedding—they both autographed each of the cards for the individual boxes of cake to be given to the wedding guests.

The sun finally came through the clouds and by late afternoon clear skies and warm southerly winds had chased away the dreary drizzle of the morning.

The gates to the White House grounds were left wide open and crowds ambled around the grounds, casting curious glances through the East and Blue Room windows, which were decked with foliage.

Anyone could come through the gates and up the wide, asphalt drive and by six o'clock a jolly, good-natured gathering of several hundred had congregated on the lawn up to the very doors of the White House.

The democratic lot was made up of a sampling of every walk of American life, from the ragged street urchin to the well-to-do merchant and his wife. They stood quietly watching with deep interest as the wedding guests arrived.

Suddenly the strains of the wedding march floated through the open windows, and at the same moment came the sound of cannons in the Navy Yard booming out a Presidential salute and the merry peal of church bells and whistles throughout the city.

It was seven o'clock, and inside the White House the President was slowly coming down the western staircase with his tall, willowy young bride on his arm. There were no attendants.

The wedding guests awaited them in the Blue Room, which had been transformed into a bower of flowers and foliage for the occasion.

Hiding the three large windows at the south of the oval room was a background of rich green foliage. Tall waving palms touched the ceiling, and tiered below were variously shaded foliage plants accented by bright scarlet geraniums and white lilies.

The mantelpiece above the west fireplace was hidden by a bed of red roses in a myriad of shades, with the monogram "C-F." in white. On the opposite mantel, against a bank of red roses and purple pansies, the date "June 2, 1886" was fashioned in yellow pansies into letters nearly a foot tall.

On the hearth under the east mantel was a mass of scarlet begonias, designed to resemble a glowing fire. Centaureas scattered at the base represented ashes, and extending out from these designs was a mosaic of blossoms laid in the form of tiles.

The handsome mirrors were festooned with smilax, and the crystal chandelier and the gaslight brackets around the walls were twined with greens.

Above the door leading from the main corridor were the words "E Pluribus Unum," worked in dark blue immortelles on a deep red background. Rose garlands twined above it and the other doors.

As the bridal couple entered the Blue Room, the President nodded to Marine Band Director Sousa and the music stopped.

They took their places in the center of the room, below the gaslight crystal chandelier, which poured a flood of light on the scene.

"Tall, graceful, blue-eyed and fair, blushing like the morn beneath her misty veil," the bride leaned on the President's arm and the Rev. Byron Sunderland of the First Presbyterian Church stepped forward to meet the couple.

The bride, who had chosen her trousseau in Paris, wore a gown of corded ivory satin with trimmings of silk India muslin, crossed in Grecian folds over the front of the high corsage and fastened in the folds of satin at the left side.

Orange blossoms and leaves edged the V of the bodice and extended down the left side of the draped skirt, which opened over a fall of the soft India muslin. The three-quarter-length sleeves were edged with muslin and trimmed with small sprigs of orange blossoms.

A coronet of orange blossoms held her veil of tulle, about five yards long, which completely enveloped her, falling to the edge of the petticoat in front and extending the entire length of the court train. The bride deftly managed the voluminous veil and train so that it lay in a glistening coil at her feet during the ceremony.

She carried no flowers and wore no jewelry except her engagement ring, a setting of sapphire and two diamonds.

She wore one long, left glove and carried the right one as she stood hand in hand with the bridegroom, the President.

He was attired in a dress suit of black broadcloth with a low cut vest, patent leather shoes, and a white lawn tie. He, too, wore one white kid glove and carried the other one.

At the end of the ceremony, from which the President had omitted the word "obey" in his wife's vows, the bridegroom slipped on his wife's finger a plain, gold wedding band engraved only with the date.

With the last words of the benediction, which was pronounced by the Rev. William Cleveland, the President's brother, Mrs. Folsom stepped forward and kissed her daughter's cheek.

The President's sisters, Miss Cleveland and Mrs. H. E. Hoyt, were next to offer congratulations, followed by the other guests.

Then Sousa and the Marine Band struck up the Bridal Chorus from "Lohengrin" and the President led his wife into the East Room, and then to the family dining room where the wedding supper was served.

The dining room mantel was a solid bank of roses, and blooming plants and foliage decorated the sideboards and windows.

The centerpiece of the table was a full-rigged three-masted ship, named Hymen for the Greek god of marriage, constructed of pinks, roses and pansies. It sailed on the magnificent Monroe plateau, the mirror representing a lake. The national colors hung from the main mast, and two small, white flags, with the monogram "C-F." in gold letters, hung from the other masts.

The bride buried a pearl-handled knife deep in the rich wedding cake, and the guests toasted her health in champagne.

Cables from Queen Victoria, King Leopold of Belgium, Emperor William of Germany, the President of France and

FRANK LESLIE'S
ILLUSTRATED
NEWSPAPER

No. 1,603.—Vol. LXII.]   NEW YORK—FOR THE WEEK ENDING JUNE 12, 1886.   [PRICE, 10 CENTS.

WASHINGTON, D. C.—THE WEDDING AT THE WHITE HOUSE, JUNE 2ND—THE MOTHER'S KISS.

FROM A SKETCH BY C. BUNNELL.—SEE PAGE 261.

Mr. Grover Cleveland

and

Miss Frances Folsom,

Married,

on Wednesday, June second,

eighteen hundred and eighty-six.

Executive Mansion,

Washington.

President Diaz of Mexico were among the hundreds of congratulations that poured into the White House.

The President's gift to his bride was a superb diamond necklace, and the other gifts were rich and numerous, but at the President's request the wedding gifts were not displayed.

Many of the gifts had been selected with care to please a feminine young bride. They included a diamond spray from Secretary of the Navy and Mrs. William C. Whitney, an elegant set of silver candlesticks from Secretary of War and Mrs. William C. Endicott, a gold smelling bottle set with diamonds from Secretary of Interior Lucius Q.C. Lamar, a diamond ornament that could be worn either as a broach or a pin for the hair from Postmaster General and Mrs. William F. Vilas, and a diamond pendant from W. S. Bissell of Buffalo.

At the plate of each guest were beautiful favors, satin bags and boxes of bonbons as well as the little wedding cake boxes. On the lid was a spray of flowers, hand-painted, and the date, "June 2, 1886" in shaded lettering.

The President and Mrs. Cleveland left their guests to change into travel clothes, and the bride then rejoined her husband on the landing. Her travel ensemble was deep gray, the high collar fastened by a coquettish gray velvet bow.

After a tearful adieu between the bride and her mother, with the President gently urging his wife to come along, the couple stepped out of the window of the Red Parlor onto the south balcony. A closed carriage waited to take them to the train for Deer Park, Maryland, and a shower of rice and slippers descended on the carriage as the horses trotted off.

The bridal pair arrived at their Deer Park retreat in a drizzling rain at four o'clock in the morning. But, alas, there was no privacy for the President and his bride. Several reporters had arrived earlier.

Headlines on the front pages of newspapers during their honeymoon week announced the news: "Mrs. Cleveland Fishes." Many reporters filed daily stories about the honeymooning couple, sometimes using spyglasses to keep up with their comings and goings at the plush resort.

It was probably with joy that the President and his bride returned to Washington and retired behind the walls of the White House.

The public did not quickly come out of the rosy glow created by the wedding. Bands played romantic songs around the clock. The country had a new idol, Mrs. Cleveland. Her picture could be found in almost every home. Women wore their hair as she did—a low knot at the nape of the neck.

When the public learned she had played the piano for the President on their honeymoon, requests rained on the White House from piano makers asking permission to place a piano in the White House for her pleasure.

The repeated use of her picture in advertisements for patent medicine, perfume, candy and garments resulted in a bill being introduced in the House of Representatives on March 6, 1888, proposing to make it against the law to employ the likeness of any female in public exhibition without her written consent. However, it was never passed.

The new Mrs. Cleveland took all these attentions with grace and carried off her social responsibilities with a charm and sincerity and a commanding poise that won the hearts of the American people.

The President had ordered a house-cleaning and repainting inside and out for the bride's homecoming, but he wisely left questions of redecoration for Frances to decide.

There were few structural changes made in the mansion, however, as President Chester Arthur had completely redecorated the White House in the summer of 1882, adding a large ornate screen of Tiffany glass in the main corridor, where it remained for the next 25 years.

Frances loved flowers and the conservatory was a constant delight to her. She liked birds also and filled the private quarters of the house with song birds, mocking birds and canaries. The story is told that on one occasion the President was trying to concentrate upon a message late at night and became so distracted by the singing of a mocking bird that he called one of the White House staff to remove it to another room.

The new First Lady opened her official social program with a New Year's Day reception in 1887. One account of the affair described it as "gorgeous, gay and giddy," adding that the Executive Mansion "never looked cleaner or grander."

She gave two receptions a week, on Thursday night and on Saturday afternoon so that working women employed during the week could meet her. At one reception she shook 9,000 hands and her arms ached so that they had to be massaged. But she kept smiling and some of the women went through the line twice just to see her smile.

Just before his marriage, President Cleveland bought a private home on the outskirts of Washington where he and his wife lived much of the time except during the social season when official entertainment demanded they stay at the White House. It was actually a comfortable old farm, named Oak View but dubbed Red Top by the newspapers because of the color of the roof. The farm was stocked with animals, had a kitchen garden and a coachhouse. It also had a magnificent view of the city and was located near those famous old Georgetown Heights estates, Grasslands, Rosedale and Woodley.

Cleveland was a hard-working President but he faced a hard campaign for re-election to a second term. In the close political contest of 1888 he lost to the Republican candidate, Benjamin Harrison. But when the Clevelands left the White House, Frances promised the staff they would be back in four years. They were, with their baby daughter Ruth to share the spotlight showered on the First Family.

Another daughter, Esther, was born in 1893—the first child of a President to be born in the White House. A third Cleveland daughter, Marion, was born in 1895 while the First Family was vacationing at Buzzard's Bay, Massachusetts.

Two sons, Richard and Francis Grover, were born to the marriage after the Clevelands had left the White House and the family was living in Princeton, New Jersey.

After Grover Cleveland's death in 1908, his widow married Thomas J. Preston in 1913. She died in 1947 at the age of 82.

Lace trimmed, satin covered wedding cake boxes, each with a card bearing the signatures of both the bride and bridegroom, were among the favors given the guests at the wedding reception of President Cleveland and the former Frances Folsom.

117

The Smithsonian Institution

XIII

The Most
Brilliant
Wedding of All

Alice Lee Roosevelt - Nicholas Longworth
February 17, 1906

here had never been a wedding in the White House like that of Alice Lee Roosevelt to Representative Nicholas Longworth of Ohio. But, then, there had never been a President's daughter quite like Alice.

She was accustomed to the spotlight. Shortly after the Theodore Roosevelts moved into the White House in 1901 following the death of President McKinley, Miss Roosevelt made her debut at a White House party and immediately attained unparalleled popularity. (That debut, however, was not all she had hoped for. Alice had to settle for fruit punch instead of champagne at the party, and a dance instead of a cotillion.)

Whatever she did was followed with great interest by her many admirers. Songs were written about her. "Alice blue," a greenish-blue color she liked, was worn by maids and matrons throughout the country. She was known as "Princess Alice."

Alice Lee Roosevelt and Nicholas Longworth standing before Bishop Satterlee who performed their marriage ceremony. Drawn by H. G. Dart for Leslie's Illustrated Weekly.

Her "eligible friends" were too numerous to count. For at least two years before her marriage there was rarely an evening when some party was not given in her honor. She was starred at the Mardi Gras in New Orleans, at the Chicago Horse Show and at the St. Louis World's Fair. She christened the Kaiser's yacht "Meteor" and sat in a box with white-haired Mark Twain at Yale University's bicentennial celebration.

Her marriage at 22 to the sought-after 36-year-old Congressman from Ohio caught and held the interest of the entire nation. Newspapers were full of the story. There was nothing else but news of her wedding on the front page of the *Washington Post* the day following the ceremony. Reporters flocked to Washington. Gifts poured in by the hundreds. Even the winter day Alice chose for the wedding—February 17, 1906— turned out to be springlike.

This photograph of Alice Lee Roosevelt shows how she looked during her first year in the White House.

The East Room of the White House had been turned into a beautiful bridal setting for what was the most exciting and probably the most expensive wedding ever held in the Executive Mansion.

The four windows on the east side of the room were draped with a large lambrequin of old gold plush with curtains on either side. Large ropes of smilax and bunches of Easter lilies hung from every possible loop and border.

Two semicircular steps led to an elevated platform in front of the windows. A rich Oriental rug covered the platform. At the top of the steps stood a *prie-dieu* upholstered in white cloth tied with white satin ribbons and filled with bride's roses and lilies.

Forming a background between the platform and the windows were masses of palms and smilax with a great bunch of Easter lilies in the middle. On either side stood a large Satsuma vase filled with Easter lilies and beyond each of them a vase with Easter lilies set upon a pedestal.

Other state rooms of the presidential mansion were equally elaborate in decorations. In the niches of the main corridor green palms and other tropical plants formed a background for mauve azaleas. In the Green Room light pink carnations mingled with delicate green ferns. In the Blue Room were vases of Easter lilies with asparagus ferns, and palms were placed in the window recesses. Vases filled with red roses and asparagus fern decorated the Red Room; in the State Dining Room were vases of bride's roses on the mantel and vases of American Beauty and bride's roses with fern on the table.

The rooms were virtually furnished with flowers because all the furniture including rugs had been removed to provide more space for the large number of guests.

Extra help was hired or brought from various government departments to help take care of the guests. The police detail numbered 72. Ten extra men were brought in to help open the carriages of the guests; 11 men and 15 women staffed the East Terrace cloak boxes. A total of 145 carriages arrived at the east entrance and unloaded at the rate of five a minute.

As the first of the 680 guests began to arrive, an hour early for the 12 o'clock noon ceremony, they were shown their places in three areas roped off by white satin ribbon. Two of the ribbons formed an aisle, carpeted in green, from the door of the East Room to the improvised altar.

Between the aisle and the west wall of the room was another rope reserving a section for members of the Cabinet and their families, and members of the Diplomatic Corps and their families. The important people were placed as near the platform as possible; people who came late were permitted to stand in the main vestibule and along the north side of the main corridor.

The Marine Band, its members in gold braid dress uniforms with scarlet jackets, played wedding music in the lobby under the direction of William H. Santelman as the guests flowed in. The program included:

Grand March—"Tannhauser"	Wagner
Overture—"Jubilee"	von Weber
Ballet Music and Wedding Procession	
from the Opera *Feramors*	Rubinstein
(a) Dance of the Bayaderes No. 1 Moderato	
(b) Candle-dance of the Brides of Kashmir 'L'istesso tempo et Moderato con moto	
(c) Dance of the Bayaderes No. 2, Allegro vivace assai	
(d) Wedding procession. Moderato	
Polonaise "Military"	Chopin
Waltz—"The Debutante"	Santelman
Serenade from Symphony "Rural Wedding"	Goldmark
Fleurette	Herbert
Hungarian Rhapsody No. 2	Liszt
March—"Bride Elect"	Sousa

Fifteen minutes before the ceremony was to begin the guests began pushing and straining to see the altar and those in the front ranks. One woman fainted and had to be carried from the room. She quickly regained consciousness and returned to her place. The windows were opened to cool the rising temperature.

At five minutes before noon, Mrs. Roosevelt, the stepmother of the bride, a younger daughter, Ethel, and three sons, Kermit, Archibald and Quentin, came down the marble staircase and entered the East Room. They were accompanied by two White House military aides.

The First Lady wore a gown of heavy cream-colored brocade with a raised design of blue and brown figures interlaced with threads of gold.

As soon as they were in their places on the left side of the platform the Episcopal Bishop of Washington, the Right Rev. Henry Yates Satterlee, and the Rev. Roland Cotton Smith were escorted by a military aide to the altar.

Immediately behind them came the bridegroom and his best man, Thomas Nelson Perkins. Representative Longworth, a stocky figure of medium height with only a fringe of hair on his head, wore the conventional costume for afternoon weddings. His black frock coat was unbuttoned, showing a white Marseilles waistcoat. His trousers were the darkest shade of gray, his gloves of heavy white doeskin, and his shoes of patent leather. In the center of his pearl gray silk cravat tied in the pouf style was a moonstone stickpin. A large white carnation was pinned in the buttonhole of his left lapel.

Promptly at noon, Alice Roosevelt, escorted by the President, who looked very formal, descended in the elevator at the west end of the main corridor.

Her gown was a magnificent creation of cream satin, princess in style with an 18-foot-long train of silver brocade. The yoke and elbow sleeves were of lace that had been part of her mother's wedding dress. The tulle veil, worn off the face over her dark pompadour-style hair, was caught with a coronet of orange blossoms. Clusters of the same flowers nestled in the lace on her shoulders. Her only jewelry consisted of a necklace of diamonds, a gift from the bridegroom, and a diamond brooch, a gift from her father.

She carried a cascading bouquet of orchids, tied with white chiffon satin ribbon that fell in a shower to the hem of her gown.

Eight ushers escorted the bride and her father down the long red-carpeted corridor to the green-carpeted aisle and then to the altar.

The ushers, many of whom had been Nick's classmates at Harvard, were Buckner Wallingford, Quincy Adams Shaw, Jr., Larz Anderson, Guy Norman, Francis R. Bangs, Frederick Winthrop, Viscount Charles de Chambrun, the bridegroom's brother-in-law, and Theodore Roosevelt, Jr., brother of the bride.

As the Marine Band played the magnificent march from "Tannhauser," Alice, with her hand on the arm of her father, entered the East Room with her head high and her blue eyes on the man who waited for her.

As the music stopped and Bishop Satterlee came to the center of the platform, the President stepped back. The bride, taking the arm of the bridegroom, stepped upon the dais facing the Bishop. Her cousin, Franklin Delano Roosevelt, who had been married the preceding year in a wedding at which the President had given the bride away, stepped forward and straightened the bride's train.

When Bishop Satterlee asked, "Who giveth this woman away," the usually booming voice of the President was barely audible to the silent audience as he responded, "I do." He placed his daughter's hand in the hand of the bridegroom, gave the bride's bouquet to his other daughter, Ethel, and took his position beside his wife.

There were no bridesmaids, maid of honor or flower girls to share the spotlight with the indomitable Alice.

As soon as the ceremony was over, Alice's usual bubbling charm took over. The President and First Lady were the first to congratulate the young couple and Teddy Roosevelt was all smiles as he pumped the hand of his new son-in-law. Then he and Mrs. Roosevelt received the guests in the Blue Room, after they had filed by the East Room altar to congratulate the young couple.

Alice Lee Roosevelt in a stately, dignified pose at the White House in 1903.

While the guests gathered in the dining room for the wedding breakfast catered by Rauscher, Alice and her special friends went to the small family dining room off the State Dining Room. Charlie McCawley, the President's military aide, offered his sword to her and she gaily accepted it to cut the bride's cake.

She asked another military aide, U. S. Grant, III, grandson of the former President, to bring her some of the telegrams that had come in. Merriment reigned as she read the congratulatory messages, many of which were humorous. One from Emily Sears, a Boston friend, read, "I always knew old Nick would get you."

"The Brothers Immediate" of the Porcellian Club at Harvard had come down for the wedding of their fellow member and in keeping with tradition brought their own steward, whom

123

the President put in charge of the champagne. Toward the end of the breakfast, the President invited all the members of the club to join him in the private dining room and they held a very pleasant reunion. For nearly an hour the 40 men sang college songs, with the President's booming voice often heard above the others.

By three o'clock all the guests had left and Alice changed into her travel costume. At four-thirty she and Nick left the house by the south entrance, the President and his family and a few others escorting them to an automobile. The conventional rice was thrown and a slipper was placed on top of the automobile for good luck.

The bridal couple motored to Friendship, the John R. McLean estate at the edge of Washington (now McLean Gardens on Wisconsin Avenue), where they stayed a few days before going to Cuba for their honeymoon.

The bride's going away dress was a beige costume, which she later described as "hideous and unbecoming." However, there was one dress in her trousseau, assembled in New York, which she treasured very much. It was a yellow satin with brilliants on the waist and on a panel down the front. She wore it 25 years later on her silver wedding anniversary with her hair again in the pompadour style of her wedding day.

The wedding was impressive and dignified. Adding to the splendor of the event were the lovely gowns of the women who were guests. The *Washington Post* carried a list of the prominent guests and a description of what each woman wore. There was much gold and silver braid, laces and embroidery; gowns with and without trains; gowns long and short.

Mrs. Charles W. Fairbanks, wife of the Vice-President, wore violet chiffon with a flower hat to match. Baroness Hengelmuller, wife of the Austrian Ambassador, wore a Parisian voile princess gown of pink coral trimmed in gold. Nellie Grant Sartoris, who had been married in the White House 32 years before, looked elegant in gray chiffon velvet, a lace toque and gray furs.

Attracting as much attention as the clothes were the gifts that poured in for weeks prior to the ceremony. Probably no bride up to that time had received so many gifts from friends, foreign potentates and unknown admirers.

King Edward sent a snuff box of blue and gold enamel with his miniature on it. The Kaiser sent a bracelet set with a miniature of himself. The King of Italy sent a mosaic table so large that the bride said later she had never been able to use it in any of the rather small houses that she had lived in.

The French government sent a handsome Gobelin tapestry. The Empress Dowager of China gave eight rolls of cloth, brocaded in gold that never tarnishes, with the Chinese shu sign of longevity worked into the design. She also sent two rings, a pair of earrings, some white jade, a white fox coat and an ermine coat.

From the Republic of Cuba came the most cherished gift of all—a necklace of 62 matched pearls with a diamond clasp. The bride wore it proudly throughout the years that followed. The government of Cuba, mindful of the war with Spain eight years earlier and the capture of San Juan Hill by the Rough Riders led by Theodore Roosevelt, appropriated $20,000 to buy the gift.

Alice never saw many of the gifts that came in. They were handled by the White House staff and acknowledged by the social secretary, Belle Hagner. They came from thousands of individuals and firms. Some were gorgeous and others ridiculous. A paper of pins came from one woman, a hogshead of popcorn from a manufacturing firm, a box of snakes from a collector, innumerable fancy cakes, gold, silver, cutglass, diamonds, pearls, household items such as brooms and feather dusters, washing machines, furniture, heirlooms and books by the score.

Fifteen reporters were invited to cover the wedding in the East Room, twelve women and three men. Scores more were in Washington to write about the event. One of them was humorist Irvin S. Cobb, who said in an interview years later with Edward Folliard of the *Washington Post*, "That was a great story. There must have been a million reporters in town. They came from all over the country and one of them came here from London. . . ."

The interest in Princess Alice, he said, was caused not alone by the fact that she was the daughter of President Roosevelt but because of those "stories" that were being whispered about her.

125

"Alice had been seen to smoke cigarettes. It was alleged that she would take a cocktail. But worst of all, she had been seen out in Rock Creek Park in riding breeches. She was thus exposing those things that were presumed to exist between the pelvis and the instep but which people never admitted existed in those days," Cobb added.

Several years later, when William Howard Taft was President, Alice visited the White House and showed a friend exactly the spot on which she stood while being married.

"It was here," she said, planting a foot firmly on the spot, "and I remember looking up and seeing Nick and thinking how hopelessly Middle West he did seem."

Middle West in appearance or not, it was obvious to all who met them that she was very much in love with him. During the months before her marriage, she accompanied Nick to the Capitol almost daily, even on her birthday a few days before the wedding. She enjoyed sitting in the gallery and listening to the debate for she knew the participants and the issues.

Alice's relationship with her father was one of deep devotion. Her mother had died when she was two days old and her father remarried when she was three so she had no consciousness of having a stepmother. But it was her father who made the greatest impression on her young years.

As a child, she was shy and sensitive, the one member of the family who did not particularly enjoy the strenuous exercise imposed on the children by the outdoor-loving father, whether they were in Washington or spending the summer at Sagamore Hill on Oyster Bay.

Like it or not, Alice went along with the daily swims in Oyster Bay, the handicap races and the rowing picnics. These endeavors led by an enthusiastic and fearless father developed both courage and character in his five children.

Alice, the eldest child, learned to invent her own games of skill and daring. And she learned how to win her way with a doting father. Because their dispositions were so much alike, they clashed on occasions. After she was told, "You shall not smoke under our roof," Alice puffed her cigarettes "on the roof, up the chimney, out-of-doors and in other houses." But she didn't give up smoking.

Her antics included keeping a pet green snake named Emily Spinach after they moved into the White House. She carried it with her frequently and the snake caused commotion after commotion when she took it with her on a series of visits in New England.

At one house it got lost in the folds of the drawing room curtains; at another it shed its skin under the bed and was found lying on top of the bed. It met its end, however, at the Walter Damrosches' in Bar Harbor, where Alice found it dead on the roof outside her window.

Next to having fun, politics was her one great interest. She was interested in everything that concerned her father and could hold her own in conversation with any of the politicians who came to call at the White House.

She delighted in using her own persuasive powers to help her father win support for his projects and ideas. When she was 17, at one of the first dinner parties she attended in the White House she was seated between "Uncle" Joe Cannon, Speaker of the House, and another Congressman. She had been told to extract from them a hardwood floor for the East Room, then carpeted. Her efforts coupled with her father's brought success, for Congress soon appropriated a large sum for repairing and refurnishing the mansion and for building a new west wing for offices.

By her own admission, however, Alice's main preoccupation in those days was having a good time and to her this usually meant "total irresponsibility and perpetual rushing from place to place from one amusement to another."

While Alice was having fun, her heroic father was adding to his own laurels as a "do-something" President. He had signed the Reclamation Act fostering a great conservation movement. He had settled the Alaskan boundary dispute and a coal strike. Perhaps most important, he had secured the passage of the Isthmian Canal Act, authorizing construction of a waterway across Panama. When the Republic of Panama seceded from Colombia, he recognized her independence, thus assuring the building of the canal. And in late January 1905, he originated the move toward peace in the Japanese-Russian war that led to the signing of the peace treaty in Washington the following September.

Pictures from Harper's Weekly, February 17, 1906 showing scenes on the Philippine trip which preceded the announcement of Alice Roosevelt's engagement to Nicholas Longworth.

About this time the President decided to send Secretary of War William Howard Taft on an inspection trip to the Philippines followed by a good will mission to the Orient. Alice was to go with him.

This delighted her greatly and compensated for her disappointment at not being able to go to England for the coronation of King Edward because of the great discussions over what rank should be accorded a president's daughter upon such an occasion.

At the end of June 1905, three months after her father's inauguration for a second term, the mission set out. As the President's daughter and hostess to many VIPs who welcomed the group as their train moved across the country to the West Coast, Alice kept the mission in the news.

Among the large delegation of Senators, Representatives and their wives was a young bachelor from Cincinnati, Representative Nicholas Longworth. He was already one of Alice's close friends and shared the gay social life she enjoyed in Washington.

While they were together on the good will mission, rumors of their engagement began to circulate. The two spent so much time together that Taft would ask her from time to time, "Alice I think I ought to know if you are engaged to Nick." She always replied, "More or less, Mr. Secretary, more or less."

One rumor was that Nick had put the question to her as they were entering the door of the Empress Dowager's palace in Peking and that her affirmative answer came at the same spot as they emerged.

This, like so many other rumors, was not true, Miss Roosevelt said. However, it was true that she jumped fully clothed into a swimming pool on the deck of the ship and challenged some of her friends to do likewise. Irrepressible Alice said she felt it her "pleasurable duty" to stir up her fellow voyagers and this was one way of doing it. Another way was to smoke in their presence.

Miss Roosevelt's own version of their engagement was that "we had not been back from the trip long before Nick and I decided we were engaged and that we might as well announce our engagement as the papers were daily doing it for us."

The story is told that when the *Chicago Tribune* sent its Washington bureau a wire: "Is Alice Roosevelt engaged, or is she not?" the badgered bureau chief wired back: "She went out driving with Nick Longworth this afternoon without a chaperone. If they are not engaged, they ought to be." The newspaper announced the engagement in the morning paper. That afternoon, the President and Mrs. Roosevelt announced it.

"I remember that I felt shy and self-conscious about telling the family that we were engaged," Mrs. Longworth wrote later in her memoirs, *Crowded Hours*. "I had the perfectly unwarranted feeling that they might be sentimental about it. I put off telling for a long time. Finally, one evening I followed Mother into her bathroom and told her the news while she was brushing her teeth, so that she should have a moment to think before she said anything. Nick, meanwhile, with great formality was announcing it to Father in the study."

She said she could not remember when she first met her husband. Longworth was a member of an old, respected family in Cincinnati that had long been friends of the Roosevelts, and he had visited in their home when Alice was a little girl.

When they became engaged, he gave her a ring set with three pale rubies and a small diamond. Alice thought the ring unattractive and stopped wearing it shortly after their marriage, explaining to her husband she did not like rings. She continued, however, to wear the plain gold wedding band he slipped on her finger at the wedding.

When the couple returned from their Cuban honeymoon, they lived in a handsome four-story brick house at Eighteenth and I Streets, in Northwest Washington. Sightseeing stages stopped there and their passengers were invited in by Alice, who allowed them to wander around, have tea, and sometimes depart with a souvenir. Mrs. Longworth confessed later the tourists gave her a good excuse for not having "at homes," but she finally ended these sorties by pretending not to be at home when sightseers rang the bell.

In June of 1906 the Longworths took a second honeymoon, this time to Europe, where they were entertained by diplomatic and royal society for two months.

They attended a dinner in honor of King Edward and Alice sat next to him. He later attended a reception given for them by Ambassador and Mrs. Whitelaw Reid in Dorchester House, London, and they were presented at court.

At Kiel, the Kaiser gave a dinner for them and they had tea with him on the yacht that Mrs. Longworth had christened four years earlier. In Paris, they were the guests of President Fallieres at a brilliant dinner, and saw a performance by the royal Cambodian dancers brought to Paris by the King of Cambodia. They toured France, Belgium and the Rhine country by automobile and ended the round with a week at Bayreuth attending the Wagner Music Festival.

Before her marriage, Alice had little interest in music. When she had to attend a concert, she took along a book and read until her father ordered her to put it away. But her husband was a talented musician who played the violin and several other instruments. At their home in Cincinnati they often had chamber music, which she learned to enjoy.

Alice remained her fun-loving self after marriage and her national popularity seemed not to wane. As part of her fun as a young married with a love for parties she organized a "Night Riders" group. If there was not a party on or if the one she was attending grew dull, Alice might gather up several of the group's members and ride off to the home of a chosen friend. There on the lawn, whether the hour was ten or two o'clock, the group would set up howls and cat calls until the house was opened and they were invited in.

Archie Butt, who was military aide to President Taft and had also served on President Roosevelt's staff, was a member of the Night Riders. He wrote that at first there was some criticism of the group but eventually the highest social honor one could have was a raid from the Night Riders led by Alice.

There was a cheering section for Alice almost everywhere she went. One afternoon a fire broke out in her neighborhood. At its height, she approached the scene and as soon as the crowd spotted her, a cheer went up and she held a reception right there on the sidewalk.

Her interest in politics continued after her marriage and grew stronger as her husband gained prominence as a political leader. In 1910 there was talk among Ohio Republicans of choosing Nick as their nominee for Governor. This neither

Alice's wedding bouquet made by Z. D. Blackistone, Washington florist.

Alice nor Nick wanted because he was enjoying his work in Congress, where he was gaining in experience and seniority.

Alice, who was still smoking cigarettes and aware of the disapproval expressed by many who knew it, jokingly threatened that rather than permit Nick to be nominated for Governor she would smoke in the streets and thereby defeat his nomination. This did not become necessary, however. A dark horse, Warren Gamaliel Harding, was nominated.

Nick was returned to Congress year after year by his Ohio district, and later was elected Speaker of the House of Representatives.

Alice spent more and more time in the House and Senate galleries listening to the debate and watching the maneuvering on legislation. Many were the stories told in Washington dramatizing the interest of Theodore Roosevelt's daughter in what went on in Congress. One was that not long after her marriage she was giving a luncheon party, and in the middle of it someone called her to say that an important issue had come up in the Senate. Alice grabbed a hat, offered an apology to her guests and left them to finish the party without a hostess. Whether true or not, her interest was that intense.

When she was 41, Alice Longworth became a mother. She named her daughter Paulina after her favorite Biblical character, the Apostle Paul.

Paulina's quiet life was in marked contrast to that of her mother's. She married Alexander McCormick Sturm, whose death left her a widow at the age of 26. She herself died five years later, in 1956, leaving a young daughter, Joanna Sturm, who lives with Mrs. Longworth.

Princess Alice continued to live in Washington after her husband's death in Aiken, South Carolina, on April 9, 1931. Now 82, she resides in a handsome house on Massachusetts Avenue in Washington and reigns as a grande dame—a vivacious, vivid, much-quoted figure on the social and political scene. And with her erect carriage, her quick step and lively conversation she appears decades younger than her years.

The Washington Post.

WASHINGTON, WEDNESDAY, NOVEMBER 26, 1913—TWENTY-TWO PAGES.

TWO CENTS

NATIONS OF ALL THE WORLD DO HOMAGE TO
WHITE HOUSE BRIDE AS SHE TAKES SOLEMN
VOWS AMID SCENES OF UNEQUALED SPLENDOR

W. FINLEY DEAD

……'s Famous President Victim of Apoplexy.

LESS THAN SIX HOURS

DASH AWAY IN A CAR

Mr. and Mrs. F. B. Sayre Flee in Tumulty's Machine.

POLICE BLOCK THE CHASE

SPEND HONEYMOON ABROAD.

WHITE HOUSE CATS DELUDE THEM

INDEX TO TODAY'S ISSUE

THE NATION'S DAUGHTER-BRIDE

C. EDMONTON

Deserts Gilded Portals of White House to Rule Humble Home as Mrs. Francis Bowes Sayre.

Bride Cuts the Cake; Sister Gets Ring; All Dance the Tango

Merry Doings at White House by Bridal Party After Formal Guests Are Gone—Miss Margaret Wilson
Next Bride, According to Superstition—Diamond Pendant Bridegroom's Gift.
Couple Whirled Away in Automobile.

PRESIDENT WILSON GIVES DAUGHTER IN MARRIAGE TO FRANCIS B. SAYRE

**Surrounded by Throng of Notables She Repeats
Service in Firm, Clear Voice—Radiant,
Beautiful and Unshaken by Scene.
Diplomats Add Brilliancy
to Ceremony.**

East Room a Fairyland

Wedding Party Enters

President Gives the Bride

MISS WILSON GOES TO MARRIAGE ALTAR IN A SCENE OF DIGNITY AND BRIDAL

XIV

The First
of the
Wilson Brides

Jessie Woodrow Wilson - Francis Bowes Sayre
November 25, 1913

oodrow Wilson was the only President to give two of his daughters in marriage in the White House.

The wedding of Jessie Woodrow Wilson to Francis Bowes Sayre was a brilliant East Room event, with the nation's highest dignitaries and the envoys of foreign courts among the guests at the late afternoon ceremony on November 25, 1913.

Jessie, the middle daughter in the Wilson trio of girls, was considered "the angel of the family." She had once wanted to be a missionary, then compromised by working hard at a settlement house in Philadelphia after her graduation from Goucher College in 1908.

Jessie met Frank Sayre through the enterprising efforts of Frank's aunt, Blanche Nevin, who had met the Governor of New Jersey and Mrs. Wilson in Bermuda and had promptly picked their daughter Jessie, sight unseen, as a good match for her "favorite nephew" Frank.

To her romantic, old ancestral home "Windsor Forges" at Churchtown, Pennsylvania, Aunty Blanche invited Frank during his spring recess from law school, and also invited Jessie and Eleanor Wilson to share the long spring weekend.

When Jessie and sister Nell stepped off the train, Frank was waiting with a horse and buggy to drive them to Windsor. Aunty Blanche's hunch was right. Frank had eyes only for Jessie, for he saw "a rarely beautiful girl, gracious and winning, of medium height, with radiant blue eyes, clusters of golden hair wound round her delicately shaped head, her countenance beaming with health and beauty. Her face was strong-featured and firm, yet withal of ethereal loveliness." Thus Frank described the lovely Jessie many years later in his memoirs *Glad Adventure* (published by the MacMillan Company, 1957).

This front page of The Washington Post on November 26, 1913 tells about the wedding of Jessie Woodrow Wilson to Francis Bowes Sayre.

Letters followed the three happy spring days spent at Windsor, and by the fall of 1912, when Frank had won a position in the office of the New York County District Attorney, he was a regular caller at the Wilson home on Cleveland Lane in Princeton, New Jersey.

One beautiful Indian summer Sunday afternoon, Frank and Jessie drove "behind a very understanding horse" out in the golden countryside. There Frank told Jessie that he believed God had made them for each other and had brought them together. He asked her to share his life, but Jessie was too moved to give an immediate reply. She asked for time to think it over.

The following Tuesday Frank called at the Wilson home, with high hopes. Jessie met him at the door, pulled a gray cloak around her and led Frank out into the foggy evening and down a secluded pathway. With few words they plighted their troth, under a misty harvest moon. When they were choosing their wedding date the following autumn, they wanted it to be a Tuesday—the day that marked their engagement.

The Wilsons all loved Frank and even the President had to admit, "He's almost good enough for Jessie." Within this close-knit family circle the President could put aside, momentarily, the nation's problems long enough to recite limericks, or spend an evening reading aloud from Wordsworth or some other favorite author, or play a gay game of charades.

Since Frank bore a resemblance to the President, he could slip into Washington for visits with Jessie and be accepted as a Wilson cousin by the ever-present reporters. Sometimes the pair would meet on the banks of the C & O canal and paddle off in a canoe for the afternoon, unseen by the reporters. Jessie's radiant glow was a telltale mark of the romance.

Jessie's wedding was the most important social event of the new administration in the White House. Though Jessie and Frank didn't want a big wedding, they found it impossible to follow their personal wishes without hurting too many feelings. So eventually the wedding guest list was limited only by the size of the East Room.

With her mother and Eleanor, Jessie went to New York to order her trousseau and her bridesmaids' dresses. For the bridesmaids she selected four shades of rose charmeuse, ranging from palest pink for her sister Margaret, the maid of honor, to deep rose for Eleanor. The other bridesmaids were to be Mary White of Baltimore, Adeline Mitchell Scott of Princeton and Marjorie Brown of Atlanta.

The gowns were designed with Elizabethan ruffs of silver lace and the skirts were draped to show a daring four inches of silk stocking through silver petticoats. Little rose velvet caps wired with silver lace to stand up in the Russian fashion completed the chic bridesmaids' attire.

Wedding presents poured into the White House, including a magnificent silver service from the Senate and a beautiful diamond pendant from the House of Representatives, a tiny handbeaded purse from the bride's four-year-old cousin, handmade articles from the mountaineer women of the South whose crafts had always interested and been promoted by Mrs. Wilson, and gold coffee spoons. But some of the presents were "pretty awful" and these were kept hidden behind the door in the room where the gifts were displayed, then trotted out just in time when the donor came in sight at the wedding reception.

The President turned the Presidential yacht, the "Mayflower," over to Frank for his ushers' dinner, while Jessie gave her bridesmaids' dinner at the White House.

Frank's old friend Dr. Wilfred Grenfell had just returned from Labrador and served as the best man. The ushers were Charles Hughes, son of Justice Hughes and a law school classmate of Frank; Dr. Gilbert Horrax, a Williams College classmate from Montclair, New Jersey; Dr. Scoville Clark who had been in Labrador and Newfoundland with the bridegroom; and Benjamin Brown Burton, another Williams associate, who had accompanied Frank on an expedition to Alaska and Siberia.

On the wedding day, the bride and groom followed the old custom of not seeing each other until the ceremony.

Frank and his best man took a leisurely walk over the Fourteenth Street bridge into Virginia, arriving back just in time to dress and drive to the White House.

At the White House the guard at the front gate could not be convinced that Frank was the bridegroom. Neither Frank nor his best man carried an invitation to the wedding or identification that day of days. Frank pleaded that the wedding couldn't take place without him.

"You'll have to tell that to the Captain," said the skeptical guard. "I have my orders, and this is a very special White House occasion."

At last the Captain, summoned from the sentry box at Frank's request, listened to the likely story and, with a twinkle, let the flustered and embarrassed groom into his own wedding.

Upstairs in the White House the Wilson girls and their mother were spending the last hour before the wedding together. The sisters helped Jessie dress in the beautiful long, satin gown trimmed with rare old point lace that fell in graceful lines reminiscent of a Grecian statue so that Jessie looked half angel, half goddess.

Mrs. Wilson pinned the long tulle veil on Jessie's golden hair, which was dressed in a wide fillet around her head, and smiled into the eyes of her first daughter to leave the family nest.

Jessie's only jewelry was the gift from the groom—a diamond pendant and chain.

Then it was time for the bridal party to gather in the State Dining Room before the march down the long corridor to the East Room. The scarlet coated Marine Band struck up the familiar strains of the "Lohengrin" wedding march for the processional, then played a program of music selected by Margaret for the occasion. The program included "Marche Nuptiale" by Ethelbert Nevin, a cousin of Frank's mother.

The tall, distinguished President—looking very handsome in a dark gray cutaway—smiled gravely down on his daughter as he drew her arm through his and escorted her to the altar.

The east window of the East Room was banked with flowers and greenery, with tall candelabra on either side of the altar. A ribbon-bordered aisle led to the satin-covered *prie-dieu* that had been placed on a white vicuna rug, a wedding present from Peruvian Minister Pezet.

Of all the guests at the wedding, none deserved a place of honor more than Aunty Blanche Nevin, who sat proudly on the front row, her matchmaking dream come true. She was bedecked with her favorite serpent belt, rings, beads and bracelets, tinkling a unique accompaniment to the marriage ceremony.

The Rev. Sylvester Beach, who had been the Wilson family pastor in the Presbyterian Church in Princeton, performed the ceremony and Frank's brother, the Rev. John Nevin Sayre, gave the benediction.

Jessie's face, radiant with happiness as she pledged her vows, brought tears to Eleanor's eyes, and the Marine Band boomed out the recessional just in time to banish the bridesmaid's wistfulness.

The bridal party and President and Mrs. Wilson had supper in the dining room, and there were shrieks of merriment as Jessie cut her cake and Margaret found the ring in her slice.

Jessie started up the stairs to change to her traveling clothes, turning back to toss her bouquet to the bridesmaids clustered around the bottom of the staircase. She caught Eleanor's eye and deftly aimed her bouquet at her younger sister, who happily was marked to be the next bride.

Jessie changed into a violet going-away dress, with a violet velvet hat to match, and met Frank for a quiet get-away by the south entrance, where an unpretentious car was waiting to whisk them out of the White House drive, eluding reporters and a host of well-wishers.

The newlyweds spent the first two days of their honeymoon in Baltimore, where a friend had placed her home at their disposal. Then they returned to Washington for a Thanksgiving family dinner at the White House before sailing on the "George Washington" from New York for a European honeymoon.

They sailed home in late January and soon were installed in Williamstown, Massachusetts, where Frank would be a Williams College professor for the next three and a half years.

Jessie returned to the White House for the birth of their first child, Francis Bowes, Jr.,—the President's first grandchild— who was born on January 17, 1915. He is now the Very Rev. Francis Sayre Jr., Dean of Washington Cathedral. Another son, Woodrow Wilson, and a daughter, Eleanor, were also born to this happy marriage.

Jessie died unexpectedly in 1933. Frank Sayre, whose distinguished career in teaching and diplomacy has taken him to many countries, is now living in Washington. He married a widow, Elizabeth Evans Graves, in 1937.

Gorgeous Gowns and Priceless Jewels Add Luster to Imposing Wedding Cer

SOME OF THE NOTABLE GUESTS AT HISTORIC CEREMONY AND HANDSOME GOWNS THEY WORE

Mrs. George Howe Mrs. David Houston Mrs. Josephus Daniels Miss Lucy Burleson Mrs. T. Wilson Howe Mrs. Ruth Hall Mrs. Wm. C. Redfield Mrs. Lindley M. Garrison

WHITE HOUSE A-BLOOM

State Rooms Were Profuse With Flowers for Wedding.

LILIES CENTER OF SCHEME

Finders Stacked With Massive Palms, the Green Graduating in Both Sides With Delicate Ferns—Clusters of Dogwood on Marble Mantlepieces Add Charm to Walls With Historic Portraits.

Elegant Costumes Worn by Distinguished Guests At the Brilliant White House Marriage Ceremony

THE light colored gowns and smart frocklets were by the women were an attractive feature of the 6 o'clock ceremony at the White House yesterday, fitting well into the fair picture which the blue room presented and into the scene of greater brilliancy in the red room, where the reception was held, and the state dining room, where the supper was served at small, red-decked tables.

WHITE HOUSE WEDDING ANNOUNCEMENT CARD

The President and Mrs. Wilson have the pleasure of announcing the marriage of their daughter

Eleanor Randolph

to

Mr. William Gibbs McAdoo

on Thursday, May the seventh nineteen hundred and fourteen

Washington D C

COLOR PLAN IS DAINTY

Bridal Party's Gowns Reflect Keen Artistic Taste.

WHITE IS PREVAILING NOTE

Walless Effects Brought Out Against Satin-Paneled Walls and Gold and Blue Furniture of the Blue Room—Contrast to the Rose Tints of Dresses Worn at Miss Jessie Wilson's Wedding.

BRIDE'S TRAVELING SUIT IS BLUE. WHILE GOWNS FILL FIVE TRUN

XV

A Second Wilson Daughter Marries

Eleanor Randolph Wilson - William Gibbs McAdoo
May 7, 1914

leanor Randolph Wilson was the most joyous and fun-loving of the Wilson trio of daughters, and the second to marry.

She was supposed to be engaged when the Wilsons moved into the White House, but that alliance melted away when a tall, fascinating older widower, William Gibbs McAdoo, the Secretary of the Treasury, started making calls on the White House—to see Miss Eleanor.

At her sister Jessie's wedding, "Nell" and "Mac" had slipped away from the other wedding guests, who were celebrating in the East Room, to be alone in the oval Blue Room. There the President's dancing daughter gave Mac lessons in one-stepping and fox-trotting and carried on a gay conversation in whispered tones.

By the time Jessie and Frank had returned from their European honeymoon, Eleanor and Mac were engaged. But there had been an unfortunate change in the Wilson family situation, too. Mrs. Wilson's health was failing rapidly.

Eleanor insisted on as small and quiet a wedding as possible. Only relatives, members of the Cabinet and their wives, and her closest old friends from Princeton days were invited to the Blue Room ceremony.

To spare her mother the exhausting round of New York shops—which was so much fun for Eleanor—she was accompanied to New York for her trousseau-shopping spree by Aunt Ida, Uncle John Wilson's wife.

Uncle John had turned red with indignation when Eleanor had broken the news she was engaged, for he considered her practically one of his own, partly because she looked like his daughter who had been killed in an accident.

This page from The Washington Post of May 8, 1914, pictures some of the guests at the wedding of Eleanor Randolph Wilson to William Gibbs McAdoo and describes the gowns they wore.

When Eleanor finally managed to stammer, "But it's Mac, Uncle John," she was engulfed by a big hug.

"Thank God—I was afraid it was one of those damned young whipper-snappers!" exclaimed Uncle John, breathing a sigh of relief.

Between shopping tours and fittings, Eleanor could be glimpsed in the Senate gallery, where she listened to the debates over the Panama Canal tolls and proudly watched as Mac conferred with Senators.

As the wedding day approached, a flood of gifts came to the White House. Among Eleanor's favorites was an exquisite pearl and diamond bracelet from the Senate.

President and Mrs. Wilson gave their daughter a white enamel and wicker bedroom set; members of the Cabinet gave a set of 12 silver plates and a silver platter, each bordered in a quaint design similar to one of the old Sheffield models and marked with the bride's monogram; the House of Representatives sent a silver tea service including a tray and six pieces with a pair of silver candlelabra, with a chrysanthemum design and marked with the bride's initials. Auditors of the Treasury Department sent a pair of tall silver vases in the Paul Revere design, a replica of the famous Revere vases in the Boston Museum. These also were marked with the bride's initials.

The weather on the day of the wedding, May 7, 1914, was perfect, and the White House was decorated like a spring garden of white lilies, white roses and white lilacs.

The loveliest flowers grown in the White House conservatories and many sent to the bride throughout the day enhanced the beauty of the various state rooms. The East Room, through which the guests were conducted upon their arrival, had its gold decorations set off with great clusters of Annuciation lilies and boughs of blossoming dogwood; the Green Room was a bower of lilies and roses, and in the Red Room were American beauty roses and boughs of dogwood.

Dogwood blossoms filled the alcoves of the long corridor and the openings between the columns that separate it from the vestibule. The oak-paneled State Dining Room was set off with pink roses.

The ceremony was to be at six o'clock. Eleanor first went to her mother's room to help her dress—in creamy lace with a set of amethysts, a gift from her husband, and a bunch of violets for her corsage. Then the bride hurried back to her own room to dress for her wedding.

Eleanor had chosen a gown of heavy ivory satin, trimmed with real old point lace, and fashioned in a semi-medieval style. In the chiffon lining of the long train were sewn little bunches of orange blossoms, and she borrowed a tiny brooch from her mother to pin a piece of blue ribbon inside her wedding dress.

A caplike bridal wreath of orange blossoms held her long, draped tulle veil. She picked up her bouquet of white orchids, gardenias and lilies of the valley and joined her father, who was waiting at the top of the main staircase to escort her down the stairs.

Margaret and Jessie, the maid and matron of honor, were dressed in blue and rose organdie and carried tall, shepherds' crooks gracefully festooned with roses and lilies-of-the-valley around the handles.

But the wedding march didn't begin, and the bride and her father waited anxiously at the top of the stairs. With a frown, the President sent word to White House chief usher Ike Hoover to find out what had gone wrong.

Suddenly the Marine Band boomed out the wedding march and the bridal party swept down the staircase, with two little flower girls in lace-trimmed white dresses leading the way. They were Mac's 12-year-old daughter, Sallie, and Secretary of the Interior Franklin L. Lane's daughter, Nancy.

As they turned at the foot of the stairs and started down the corridor to the Blue Room, the bride's train flipped over, revealing the orange blossoms. Quickly Hoover leaned over, straightened the train, and the procession proceeded without losing a single measured step.

The Blue Room was banked with white lilies and white apple blossoms. The dais platform built between the bay windows overlooking the garden had been covered with blue satin to match the walls. The white vicuna rug that had adorned the dais during Jessie's wedding had been loaned to her sister for this wedding, and on the beautiful rug was placed the white satin *prie-dieu*, tied with white ribbons and white roses and lilies.

There in front of the bay windows, as Eleanor could see the soft dusk of the evening enveloping the Washington Monument and the blue Virginia hills, she promised to be Mac's "loving, faithful and obedient wife." It was the same ceremony the Rev. Sylvester Beach had performed for Jessie and Frank just a few months before.

After Dr. Beach pronounced the benediction, the bride turned, too quickly, to greet her guests and the long train twisted about her feet. The President, in high spirits, sprang forward and straightened out the tangled folds of satin, then spread it out full length upon the floor.

The bridal pair received the congratulations in the Red Room and the program of Marine Band music was almost identical to that of Jessie's wedding, for Margaret had selected it each time.

Supper was served at small tables in the State Dining Room and Eleanor cut the cake with the sword of Admiral Cary T. Grayson, Mac's best man and the White House physician. At last the bride ran upstairs to change, pausing half way up to throw her bouquet, which 12-year-old Sallie McAdoo leaped forward to catch.

The newlyweds had worked out an elaborate scheme to evade the press. Four cars were in the White House drives, stationed at various entrances, Jessie and Frank dashed out and leaped into one and three other couples got into the others.

Then as the reporters took off in mad pursuit in all directions, Eleanor and Mac slipped quietly into a small car and drove away, unnoticed. As Eleanor kissed her parents goodbye she glimpsed a little quiver of her father's eyelid and an unfamiliar firmness around her mother's mouth. Suddenly she was engulfed with the thought that she was leaving the family circle and barely were they out of sight before the bride collapsed in tears, to her husband's dismay.

Mac and Eleanor drove to the Wilsons' summer place, Harlakenden, in New Hampshire, but their privacy was short-lived. Reporters and visitors soon followed them to the quiet New Hampshire hills.

When they returned to Washington two weeks later, Eleanor's heart sank when she saw her mother, who looked so very small and very pale as she lay against the pillows in her bed.

Mrs. Wilson was overjoyed to see her daughter, smiling happily as she patted Eleanor's hand.

"I needed only to see your face, as I did Jessie's, to know that you are happy," she said.

But Ellen Axson Wilson could not recover from her illnesses, and she died on August 6, 1914.

Two daughters were born to Eleanor and Mac—Ellen Wilson and Mary Faith.

The marriage ended in divorce in 1934, and McAdoo died in 1941. Eleanor Wilson McAdoo is now living in Santa Barbara, California.

Eleanor Randolph Wilson in her bridal gown. She was married to Secretary of the Treasury William Gibbs McAdoo on May 8, 1914 in the White House. Photo by Clinedinst of Washington.

XVI

President Wilson's Bride

Edith Bolling Galt - Woodrow Wilson
December 18, 1915

Woodrow Wilson was the third President to be married while in office. He took as his bride on December 18, 1915, Edith Bolling Galt, a Virginia-born gentlewoman who had been a widow for seven years.

The widower President had first met Mrs. Galt only nine months earlier when she was in the White House for the first time. Each of them was wearing muddy shoes when they turned a corner from opposite directions in an upstairs hall at the White House.

The 59-year-old President had just returned from playing golf with Admiral Cary Travers Grayson, the White House physician. Edith had just returned from a walk in Rock Creek Park with Helen Bones, the President's cousin, who was living at the White House. Miss Bones had invited the attractive 43-year-old widow to come to the mansion for tea.

After the two men had changed from their golfing clothes and the women had cleaned the mud from their shoes, the four had tea before a glowing fire in the oval sitting room on the second floor. Mrs. Galt and the President got along beautifully from the first moment. The repeated laughter of the President and his light conversation indicated he was enjoying this visit.

It was Dr. Grayson, who was in love with and later married Altrude Gordon, Mrs. Galt's closest friend, who had brought the President and Mrs. Galt together. He had taken Helen Bones and the President's daughter, Eleanor McAdoo, with him when he called on Mrs. Galt one afternoon. The women became friends immediately.

After that, Helen and Edith shared many afternoon rides in the latter's electric car and walks in Rock Creek Park. On their next ride after Edith's first visit to the White House, the Presi-

---

Edith Bolling Galt Wilson who married President Woodrow Wilson after a courtship that began in the White House. They were married in her residence at 1308 Twentieth Street, N.W., Washington, D. C. A copy of a portrait that hangs in the White House, this portrait hangs in the late President's bedroom at the Wilson house, 2430 S Street, N.W., Washington, D. C.

145

dent came along. He sat in the front seat with the chauffeur and scarcely spoke a word. But that evening Edith went to the White House for dinner with the President and Helen. Again she saw the lines drop from his face as they sat before the fire and discussed books. On this occasion, the President read to her and Helen from one of his favorite books.

The next day, the President sent Mrs. Galt a handwritten note along with a book they had discussed. It was the first of many notes, with Helen Bones serving as courier for "The Tiger" as she called the President because he seemed "caged" in the White House.

There were also many afternoon rides in the next few weeks for the President, his cousin and Mrs. Galt.

On May 4, Edith had dinner at the White House again. For this occasion she wore an especially becoming dress of white satin with cream lace and a touch of emerald velvet at the edge of the deep square neck. The effect was not lost on the President, who scarcely took his eyes off her that evening.

After dinner the guests had coffee on the South Portico after which Dr. Grayson excused himself and left. The President's sister, Mrs. George Howe, and her daughter, Mrs. Cothran, strolled down the South Lawn with Helen Bones and Margaret Wilson. Edith and the President were left on the portico in the warm spring air.

He drew his chair close to hers, looked directly into her eyes and said, "I asked Margaret and Helen to give me an opportunity to tell you something tonight that I have already told them."

Then in quiet, emotion-filled tones he declared his love for her and his need for her at his side as he carried on the responsibilities of his office.

His words came as a shock to her. "Not having given a thought to such a development," she confessed in her book, *My Memoir*, "I said the first thing that came to my mind without thinking it would hurt him: 'Oh, you can't love me, for you don't really know me; and it is less than a year since your wife died.' "

The lonely President had a ready reply. He told her that in his position time was not measured by weeks, or months or years, but by experience.

"Since her death," he said of his first wife, who had died in the White House on August 6, 1914, "I have lived a lifetime of loneliness and heartache. I was afraid, knowing you, I would shock you. But I would be less than a gentleman if I continued to make opportunities to see you without telling you what I have told my daughters and Helen: that I want you to be my wife."

Mrs. Galt said that if the answer had to be yes or no at once, the answer would be no. They agreed to postpone the decision and continue their friendship.

The President warned her that whoever comes to the White House is discussed and that he could not protect her from gossip. However, he added, "If you care for me as I do for you, we will have to brave this; but as I cannot come to your house without increasing the gossip, you, in your graciousness, will have to come here. It is for this reason I have talked to the girls about it, so that they can safeguard you and make it possible for me to see you. They have all been wonderful about it, and tell me they love you for your own sake, but would anyway for mine."

From that moment on, their courtship was chaperoned by one of the President's daughters or his cousin as well as by the Secret Service. And the gossip which the President predicted began.

That summer the President saw her within the White House walls, on long afternoon rides, and at Harlakenden House, at Cornish, New Hampshire, the summer White House. Edith spent part of the summer there with Margaret and Helen. He joined them on weekends, and courted her in the moonlight with, as she described it later, "a Secret Service man behind every tree."

Those carefree days at Cornish banished all Mrs. Galt's doubts as to her love for Woodrow Wilson but she could not bring herself to marry him while he served as President. She promised, instead, to marry him if he were defeated for re-election in 1916.

Washington was buzzing with talk when Edith returned to the Capital in September. On her first evening back she dined at the White House, and made another decision as the President welcomed her warmly.

"I knew I could and would go to the end of the world with or for him," she related in her memoirs.

After dinner the two went for a ride with Helen on the backseat with them and the Secret Service in front with the chauffeur. The President talked of the increasing burdens of office and the threat of war. As they were returning, he said to Edith, "And so, little girl, I have no right to ask you to help me by sharing this load that is almost breaking my back, for I know your nature and you might do it out of sheer pity."

Edith threw her arms around his neck and gave him her answer. "Well, if you won't ask me, I will volunteer, and be ready to be mustered in as soon as can be."

From that moment plans for the marriage were begun.

Wilson told his two closest political advisers, Colonel Edward M. House, and his son-in-law, William Gibbs McAdoo, of his impending marriage. The two strategists feared adverse reaction at the polls if the President married so soon after his wife's death and immediately devised a plan to prevent it.

House went to the President with the story that Mary Hulbert Peck, an old friend with whom Wilson had carried on a correspondence for seven years, was going to bring out embarrassing information from the letters if rumors about the engagement proved to be true.

The President was shocked into illness. His first thought was of his bride-to-be but he could not bring himself to tell her. Instead, he sent Dr. Grayson to her with the story and an offer to release her from her promise to marry him.

Mrs. Galt was stunned and had no answer for Dr. Grayson to take back. For hours that evening, she sat trying to decide what to do. Finally, she went to her roll-top desk, took up her pen and wrote:

1308 Twentieth Street
Sept. 19, 1915

Dearest—
    The dawn has come—and the hideous dark of the hour before the dawn has been lost in the gracious gift of light.

I have been in the big chair by the window, where I have fought out so many problems, and all the hurt, selfish feeling has gone with the darkness—and now I see straight—straight into the heart of things and am ready to follow the road 'where love leads.'

How many times I have told you I wanted to help —and now when the final test has come I faltered. But the faltering was for love—not lack of love. I am not afraid of any gossip or threat, with your love as my shield—and even now this room echoes with your voice, as you plead, "Stand by me—don't desert me!"

This is my pledge, dearest one, I will stand by you —not for duty, not for pity, not for honor—but for love. And no matter whether the wine be bitter or sweet we will share it together and find happiness in the comradeship.

Forgive my unreasonableness tonight (I mean last night, for it is already Sunday morning), and be willing to trust me.

I have not thought out what course we will follow for the immediate present for I promised we would do that together.

I am so tired I could put my head down on the desk and go to sleep—but nothing could bring me real rest until I had pledged you my love and my allegiance.

Your own
Edith.

For two days she waited for a reply. At noon of the third day, Dr. Grayson came and said "I beg that you will come with me to the White House. The President is very ill and you are the only person who can help. I can do nothing."

Edith Galt went immediately to the White House. The President was in his room. On the pillow his drawn face was white, his eyes burning with pain. He held out an eager hand in welcome and she clasped it warmly. No words were needed to convey the feeling between them. She did not ask why he had not answered her letter, only if he had received it. He said he had.

Three months later, when they were on their honeymoon, she learned why there had been no reply. He pulled the letter—its seal unbroken—from his pocket and confessed that he had not opened it for fear it said she would never see him again.

He opened it and together they read the lines written so long before. He begged that it never be destroyed and it was not. Mrs. Wilson made it public years later.

After the President recovered from his illness, they decided to announce their engagement despite the political consequences.

She was having dinner at the White House on October 6 when the President's press secretary handed to reporters the announcement, which the President had typed himself.

On December 5, they announced that the wedding would be held at 8:30 on December 18 at Mrs. Galt's modest brick house in Washington.

Invitations poured in at the White House from all over the country asking the President and his bride to visit them for a honeymoon. The President announced he would appreciate it if no gifts were sent by foreign countries, towns or organizations, but this did not prevent the flow of gifts.

The Government of Brazil sent a bracelet of Brazilian jewels and a corsage of rare tropical feathers.

A scarf of unusual texture and color came from former Queen Liliwokalani of the Hawaiian Islands. Vice-President and Mrs. Marshall gave the bridal couple a Navajo Indian blanket. The Virginia delegation in Congress gave a silver loving cup. The Pocahontas Memorial Association sent a 15-inch bronze statue of Pocahontas because Edith Galt was a ninth generation descendant of the Indian princess. The citizens of Wytheville, Virginia, her birthplace and girlhood home, sent framed miniature portraits of her parents and also the President's parents. The Blackfeet Indians of Montana sent a gift of furs from 48 animals; and three girls in California sent a quantity of virgin gold from which the wedding ring was cast.

Soon after their engagement was announced, the President had a special telephone wire installed from the White House to Mrs. Galt's house so they might talk frequently and privately as the plans progressed. Ike Hoover was placed in charge of the arrangements and he even got the wedding license.

When the evening of the wedding arrived, the house was a paradise of flowers. The ceremony was performed in the front room before a window recess that had been transformed into a semi-circular bower with tier above tier of maidenhair ferns.

Overhead was a canopy of green in the form of a shell, the inner side lined with pearly blossoms of Scotch heather, symbolic of the origin of the President's forebears. Here and there in the green was placed a spray of purple orchids and on either side were great pyramids of American beauty roses. The white satin *prie-dieu* on which the couple knelt to receive the final blessing was adorned at each end with clusters of orchids, the bride's favorite flower.

As the Marine Band, in a small bedroom upstairs, played the Lohengrin wedding march, the President and Mrs. Galt walked side-by-side down the stairway lined with ferns and American beauty roses.

It was an Episcopal ceremony and at the words, "Who giveth this woman to be married?" Mrs. William H. Bolling, mother of the bride, placed her daughter's hand in that of the President. The Rev. Herbert Scott Smith, rector of St. Margaret's Episcopal Church, which the bride attended, performed the ceremony. He was assisted by the Rev. James H. Taylor, pastor of the Central Presbyterian Church, attended by the President.

The bride wore a costume of black velvet with a picture hat whose only ornament was a gourra spray on one side. The skirt was cut full and of walking length. The waist was richly embroidered in tones of blue shading from royal to delicate pastel through which ran threads of silver. The sleeves were of black net fashioned in tiny tucks with long bell-shaped cuffs of embroidered velvet that extended well over the hand, and reached the elbow in a lily sheath point. The collar, high and upstanding at the back, was of lace. She wore only one piece of jewelry, a diamond brooch given her by the President.

There were no attendants.

At the end of the ceremony the President kissed the bride and the two turned to receive the felicitations of the 50 relatives and friends, including Cabinet members, who were invited to the wedding.

The Marine Band played after the ceremony and during the supper. The menu was representative of the Virginia background of the President and his bride. It included oyster patties, Virginia ham and boned capon.

For the honeymoon trip the bride donned a handsome coat of broadtail finished with a deep band of Yukon fur with a high collar and muff to match.

A crowd of nearly 300 persons braved a bitter cold wind to stand in the street outside the Galt residence to see the President and his bride depart.

The couple boarded a train at Alexandria for the trip to Hot Springs, Virginia, where they had a suite at the Homestead Hotel. On the train that night the happy President danced a jig the full length of the car and sang "Oh, You Beautiful Doll" to his beaming bride.

The event was so thoroughly covered by the press, none of whom were admitted to the wedding, that reporters compiled an hour by hour schedule for both the President and his bride for that day and it was printed in the *Washington Post* the following day. Here is their compilation:

HER DAY

7:30 a.m.	Arose
8:00	Talked with President over private wire.
8:10	Breakfasted with mother and sisters.
8:45-9:00	Read mail.
9:30	Received a call from the President.
10:00	Conferred with modistes and milliners.
11:00	Inspected decorations.
11:30	Received calls from members of the family in town.
12:00	Dictated answer to notes of congratulations and wrote thanks for wedding gifts.
1:00 p.m.	Luncheon.
1:30	Resting.
4:30	Goes for automobile ride with President.
6:00	Returns home.
6:30	Dinner.
7:30	Starts to dress.
8:30	Married to President Wilson.
8:45	Cuts bride's cake.

HIS DAY

7:50 a.m.	Arose.
8:45	Breakfast.
9:30	Makes auto trip in downpour of rain to house of fiancée.
10:00	Goes to bank and gets money for trip.
11:00	Returned to White House.
11:30	Called secretary and cleared his desk of important mail and matters of state.
12:00	Attended christening of granddaughter (Eleanor Wilson McAdoo) in Blue Room.
1:15 p.m.	Luncheon.
2:00-3:00	Devoted an hour to memorandum to Secretary of State Lansing on this Government's reply to last Austrian note.
3:30	Received report from Secretary Lansing of visit to State Department of Baron Zwiedinik.
4:30	Slipped away for auto ride with Mrs. Galt.
6:00	Returned to White House.
7:00	Dined with family.
7:30	Started to dress.
8:20	Arrived at Mrs. Galt's home.
8:30	Married Mrs. Galt.
11:15	Left Washington for train at Alexandria; destination: Hot Springs, Va. Due to arrive at 8:15 a.m. Sunday.

Both the President and his bride came from large families and both had southern backgrounds. The President, the son and grandson of Presbyterian ministers, was born at Staunton, Virginia in a manse that has been restored and opened to the public. He practiced law in Atlanta, Georgia, before he became a professor of history at Bryn Mawr College. He went on to become president of Princeton University and then Governor of New Jersey before being President of the United States.

Edith Galt was the seventh in a family of 11 children born to a Wytheville, Virginia, circuit court judge. At 18, she went to visit an older sister in Washington and met jeweler Norman Galt, a cousin of her sister's husband. Four years later they were married and had six years together before his death in

153

January 1908. As a widow, Edith Galt served as head of the jewelry store her husband had owned.

When the President and Edith returned to the White House from their honeymoon in January 1916, she moved her three choice possessions into the White House: a piano, a sewing machine and a mahogany roll-top desk. In the war years her sewing machine became a work center for a Red Cross production circle.

From the very beginning, Edith Galt Wilson was the President's confidante, and as war pressures mounted he turned more and more to her. Many nights they sat together past midnight reading decoded cables to and from Europe.

After the war ended, she became the first First Lady to travel abroad while her husband was in office when she accompanied Mr. Wilson to Europe for the Versailles Peace Conferences and visits with the Allies.

At Versailles special arrangements were made to allow her to sit behind heavy red brocade curtains and listen to the speeches and the voting on the Covenant of the League of Nations.

After the conferences, she was at the President's side when he took the League of Nations issue to the people on a cross-country speaking tour, hoping to win support that would influence Congress to ratify the treaty.

In Colorado the President collapsed and was brought back to the White House where he suffered a stroke. During this long illness, Edith Wilson shut out the world from his sickroom. She met the reporters and government officials, summed up the problems and carried only those she considered most pressing to the President's bedside.

She was criticized by some who called her "Mrs. President" and charged her with trying to "run the government." The critics dubbed the last 18 months of Wilson's eight years in office "Mrs. Wilson's Regency." She referred to it as "my stewardship" and insisted she had made no decisions on her own.

Wilson was never well again but his health did improve. When he left office, he bought his wife a house at 2430 S Street, N.W., in Washington. It was there he died on February 3, 1924. Mrs. Wilson continued to live in the same house and was almost 90 when she died on December 28, 1961, the 105th anniversary of his birth.

Their house is maintained as a national shrine by the National Trust for Historic Preservation, and is open to the public daily from 10 a.m. to 4 p.m. Visitors may see many of the wedding gifts received by the President and Edith, including a handsome Gobelin tapestry given them by the French Government.

President Woodrow Wilson who gave two daughters and a niece White House weddings and was then married himself in a ceremony away from the White House.

Edith Bolling Galt Wilson in one of the elegant costumes from her trousseau.

XVII

A Wartime Wedding

Alice Wilson - Isaac Stuart McElroy, Jr.
August 7, 1918

The wedding of Alice Wilson, niece of President Woodrow Wilson, to the Rev. Isaac Stuart McElroy, Jr., on August 7, 1918, was the third held in the White House during the Wilson administration.

It was an eight o'clock ceremony at the end of a long, hot summer day. It was a very small, formal wedding because the White House was in mourning for World War I. Held in the Blue Room, the brief ceremony was witnessed by the President and Mrs. Wilson and only a dozen guests.

Alice, the daughter of Mr. and Mrs. Joseph R. Wilson of Nashville and Baltimore, had planned to have a big wedding in October in Baltimore and have Uncle Woodrow over to show him off to all her friends. But the President persuaded Alice to come to the White House for her wedding because he didn't have time to attend a wedding in Baltimore.

First Lady Edith Wilson, the President's second wife, took entire charge of the planning of the wedding, and loaned the bride a coronet of rare old point lace to which a voluminous double tulle veil that swept into a train was attached.

It was the hottest summer day the Washington weather bureau had recorded in 40 years, but a storm broke at six o'clock—just as the bride was posing for pictures in her wedding gown on the south portico—and the wind whipped her veil around a column before she could dash inside.

The storm cooled off the blistering temperatures, and it was delightfully cool by eight o'clock. Because of the war, anti-German feelings ran high throughout the country and even music by German composers was being banned from many war-

Alice Wilson, niece of President Woodrow Wilson, who was married to the Rev. Isaac Stuart McElroy, Jr., in the White House on August 7, 1918.

time weddings. But Alice liked the traditional "Lohengrin" and Mendelssohn wedding marches, and so they were played for her wedding by the Marine Band.

The President and the First Lady led the bridal procession down the stairs, followed by the bridegroom's sister, Mrs. Martin Crook, who was matron of honor.

Then came Alice on the arm of her father, the President's brother, Joseph Wilson.

The bride, who had chosen her trousseau carefully to fit the needs of a missionary's wife, wore an ankle-length gown of white georgette over ivory satin, hand-embroidered with beads by a Baltimore dressmaker. She carried a shower of bride's roses and lilies-of-the-valley.

Again the little white satin *prie-dieu* with white satin embroidered pillows was placed in front of a flower-studded background in the Blue Room. The white phlox and white hydrangeas had been gathered from the White House greenhouses in the morning.

The bridegroom and his best man, M. R. Turnbull of Richmond, Virginia, entered from the Red Parlor and were waiting with the bridegroom's father, the Rev. I. S. McElroy of the Presbyterian Church of Columbus, Georgia, who performed the ceremony.

After the double ring vows were exchanged, the President and Mrs. Wilson led the way to the State Dining Room, where pink roses studded the fern-banked mantels and mounds of pink roses were on either side of the white wedding cake centering the long table.

There were only 16 at the merry dinner for the bridal pair— when the heavy burden of the war was, momentarily, laid aside —and then the bride went upstairs to change into her going-away costume.

For traveling to their honeymoon retreat in the mountains of Virginia, the bride wore a chic costume of dark brown georgette with a dark brown velvet hat trimmed with dark blue burnt ostrich feathers. The ensemble had been made to suit the bride's original fall wedding plans.

From their mountain honeymoon the McElroys went on to White Sulphur, where the bridegroom was the pastor of the Presbyterian Church for the following year. Then in 1919 the couple left for a five-year missionary stay in Japan. Alice's beautiful wedding gown, the very height of fashion, traveled many thousands of miles and served many occasions for her new life as a missionary's wife.

To this happy marriage were born five daughters—Jessie Woodrow, Alice Wilson, Annie Lee, Katherine Josephine and Sarah Stuart—who between them have presented the McElroys with 16 grandchildren.

It has been 48 years since this August Blue Room wedding, the last White House wedding for a relative of the President.

The McElroys now live in Richmond, and the Rev. Mr. McElroy has retired after many years in Presbyterian Church work.

But, given a second chance, would Alice Wilson McElroy choose the White House for her wedding—or advise another girl to be married in the Executive Mansion?

"No, I wouldn't," she said, speaking in her Richmond home. "Going to the White House was rather like going to grandfather's to be married—for Uncle Woodrow was more like a grandfather to me because he was 11 years older than my father.

"And, of course, the White House was in mourning during the war," she added.

"The White House belongs to the people of the United States, and I can't go back there whenever I want to, as I could to a church.

"Luci Johnson married in the church of her faith and she can go back to visit the place of her wedding whenever she chooses. I think that's best."

XVIII

Roosevelt Era Weddings

Anna Roosevelt Dall - John Boettiger
January ...., 1935
Anna Roosevelt Boettiger - James A. Halsted
November 11, 1952
Ruth Googins - Elliott Roosevelt
July 22, 1933
Faye Emerson - Elliott Roosevelt
December 3, 1944
Minnewa Bell Ross - Elliott Roosevelt
March 15, 1951
Patricia Peabody Whitehead - Elliott Roosevelt
November 4, 1960
Romelle Schneider - James Roosevelt
April 14, 1941
Gladys Irene Owens - James Roosevelt
July 2, 1957

ranklin Delano Roosevelt served longer as President than any other man and more marriages occurred in his family during his occupancy of the White House than in the family of any other President.

All five Roosevelt children—four sons and a daughter— could have had White House weddings if they had chosen. But each elected to be married elsewhere.

During the 12 years their father was President, all five were married once, and one son was married twice. All told, they have had 15 marriages among them, including those performed before, during and after their father's years in the White House.

If the President or Mrs. Roosevelt ever objected to their offsprings' many marital ventures, the objections were kept strictly within the family. One family member has said their parents were "very understanding" realizing "the times in which we lived" and didn't meddle into the romances or marital affairs of their children.

Each new son-in-law or daughter-in-law was welcomed into the family, and even when divorces came, friendships often continued.

Anna, eldest of the Roosevelt children and only daughter, was married in 1926 to New York stockbroker Curtis B. Dall. That marriage, however, was foundering when Roosevelt became President. And shortly after the inauguration, Anna and her

Air Force Colonel Elliot Roosevelt and his bride, Faye Emerson, stand on a snow bank with the Grand Canyon in the background following their marriage on an observation platform overlooking the Canyon.

161

Associated Press

children, Anna Eleanor (Sistie) and Curtis Roosevelt (Buzzie) arrived at the White House to live.

Anna had traveled with her father during the campaign. She and Betsy Cushing Roosevelt, wife of her brother James, greeted the wives of politicians who visited the campaign train and wrote the thank-you notes for all the presents given to the Presidential candidate. These gifts ranged all the way from flowers to pheasants.

Traveling on that same train was John Boettiger, a correspondent for the *Chicago Tribune*, whom Anna had met earlier in Albany when her father was Governor, and her mother had invited him to a swimming party.

Anna and John were too busy during the campaign for romance, but after she moved into the White House they became serious about each other. Much of their courting was done in the Executive Mansion, where Anna had an assortment of duties helping both her father and her mother.

She answered the mail that came in response to her mother's column in a magazine and assisted also with the social duties. She was tall, attractive with bright blue eyes and a gay wit that matched her father's. She had always been his favorite child and there was a strong bond between them.

Once after a formal White House dinner, guests were gathered in the Red Room for coffee. Anna pirouetted with a couple of dance steps as she entered the room. The President, watching the amusement, reproached her: "You know better than to be so frivolous at a formal White House dinner. I'm surprised."

Anna looked at him with a saucy grin and replied, "You ought not to be. You're responsible. You helped raise me."

Sistie and Buzzie were constantly in the news and were often photographed with their famous grandfather or romping with his black Scottie, Fala, or meeting the famous personalities who came to call. Soon they became the pets of the nation.

To give them perspective, Anna took time to write two children's books for them while she carried on her other duties. The first book, titled *Scamper*, was about a bunny rabbit that had been given to children in the White House; the second, called *Scamper's Christmas*, was about the rabbit's holiday in the mansion.

In June 1934, Anna went to Reno and obtained a divorce from her first husband. Six months later, she and John Boettiger were married in a civil ceremony in the Roosevelt home at 49 East 65th Street in New York.

Because it was a second marriage for her, and because the country was in economic decline and John was then working in New York, Anna chose a quiet home wedding and not one in the White House. The President was too busy with official duties to attend the ceremony but the bride's mother was there.

The Boettigers lived in New York, where he was assistant to the motion picture czar Will Hayes. Two and a half years later, Boettiger became editor and publisher of the *Seattle Post Intelligencer*, and he and Anna moved west.

It was in Seattle that their son John was born. He is now married and is teaching at Amherst College.

When John Boettiger went overseas during World War II, Anna returned to the White House with her three children and remained there until her father's death.

She was an "unofficial assistant" to the President and saw many of his callers, whom he did not have time to see. She sat in on discussions of the 1944 campaign and assisted in working out the travel schedules. She accompanied her father to the Yalta Conference and met the other two of the "Big Three" participants: Sir Winston Churchill and Joseph Stalin. But Anna kept no diaries and wrote no memoirs of what she saw and heard.

"I promised father if I worked with him I would not keep a diary for I wanted him to have the assurance I was not making notes of all I saw and heard," she said.

When Boettiger returned from war service, he and Anna returned to the newspaper business. Anna was co-publisher with her husband and also served as women's editor, columnist and advertising solicitor.

Her marriage with Boettiger soon took an unhappy turn and in 1949 they were divorced. Three years later she married Dr. James A. Halsted, a California physician with the Veterans Administration. Her mother and two brothers, James and Elliott, attended the quiet Unitarian ceremony at the bridegroom's ranch in the Malibu mountains near Santa Monica.

After spending two years in Iran, where he was a Fulbright exchange professor at the University of Shiraz medical school, the Halsteds returned to Washington, where he became associate chief of staff for research and education at the new VA hospital.

The Halsteds live in a house full of photographs and mementos of her famous father. Typically Rooseveltian in her energy, Anna leads a full life. She keeps up with the growing Roosevelt clan right down to the latest marriage and the newest baby. She is a member of the President's Commission on the Status of Women; on the board of the Washington Chapter of the United Nations Association; on the board of Americans for Democratic Action; and carries on some of her late mother's unfinished work in connection with the Wiltwick School in New York, which provides training and rehabilitation for emotionally disturbed children. She is more interested in social reform and progress than in politics.

Also living in Washington is Sistie, now Mrs. Van H. Seagraves, librarian at the Sharpe Health School and the mother of three children. Buzzie, who dropped the Dall name to become Curtis Roosevelt, lives in New York. He is director of information for the nongovernmental organization group at the United Nations.

The first marriage to take place in the family after the Roosevelts moved into the White House was that of Elliott, the President's second son, to Ruth Googins, of Fort Worth, Texas. It took place on July 22, 1933, five days after his divorce from his first wife, Elizabeth Donnor.

Elliott had married Elizabeth in January 1932 when he was 22 and she was 21. Early in 1933 they had a son, William Donnor Roosevelt, who now lives in New York.

Elliott met Ruth Googins at a party in Dallas following a rodeo and livestock show in the spring of 1933. Soon after the meeting he instituted divorce proceedings against Elizabeth, from whom he was then separated. A divorce was granted in Minden, Nevada, on July 18, 1933.

He married Ruth Googins in a double ring ceremony at the home of her aunt and uncle, Mr. and Mrs. George C. Swiler, at Burlington, Iowa. It was a big picturesque house overlooking the Mississippi River. Anna was the only member of the Roosevelt family to attend the ceremony.

The couple made their home on a ranch near Fort Worth, where Elliott was in the broadcasting business. President and Mrs. Roosevelt visited the couple at the ranch several times while he was in office.

A daughter, Ruth Chandler, was born to Eliott and Ruth in May 1934, and was followed by two other children, Tony and David Boynton.

In September 1940, Elliott entered the Air Force as a captain and in April 1944, Ruth sued for divorce, saying he had asked her to do so. Their children were then 9, 7 and 2.

Eight months later, at the age of 34, Eliott married a third time. His bride was the 27-year-old actress Faye Emerson, whom he had met the previous September at a dinner party in Los Angeles given by a mutual friend.

The nine o'clock morning wedding was held on a glass enclosed observation platform on the rim of the Grand Canyon. The bride said it "was probably the most beautiful wedding there ever was." The window overlooked the magnificent chasm partly concealed by blankets of snow and swirling mists. The Rev. Roger Sawyer, pastor of Williams (Arizona) Methodist Church, performed the eight-minute ceremony. The bride was attended by Mrs. Joseph B. Livengood of Los Angeles, granddaughter of the late opera star, Mme. Ernestine Schumann-Heink. Maid of honor was Elliott's 10-year-old daughter, Ruth Chandler, and best man was Jack Frye, then vice-president of Transcontinental and Western Air, Inc.

From the Yavapai observation station the wedding party went to El Tovar Hotel, scenic honeymooners' retreat a mile away. Stormbound at Kingman and unable to get to the wedding were three of Elliott's friends from Los Angeles. The weather was so bad that some guests had to walk four miles from an emergency landing of their airplane at Ashford, Arizona, before obtaining a ride with a Secret Service agent to the site of the wedding.

It was a happy marriage for Elliott and Faye for a few years. They moved to Duchess County, New York, and operated a Christmas tree farm. And they were frequent visitors to the White House.

Then early in 1949 the two parted on friendly terms and by September of that year divorce proceedings were under way.

In March 1951, Elliott and Minnewa Bell Ross, daughter of Alonzo Bell, the wealthy real estate developer for whom the swank Bel Air section of Los Angeles is named, were married in Miami. It was a double ring ceremony performed by Circuit Judge George E. Holt in the living room of the Sunset Island home Mrs. Ross had occupied since December when she went to Miami to divorce her physician husband.

Minnewa Bell and Elliott had first met during the war when she was a dinner guest of his brother and sister-in-law, John and Anne Roosevelt, who attended the wedding and also accompanied the bridal couple on their honeymoon to Cuba. This marriage of Elliott's lasted nine years. In July 1960, Minnewa filed suit for divorce in Meeker, Colorado, on charges of mental cruelty.

On November 4 of that same year, Elliott took his fifth bride, Patricia Peabody Whitehead of Phoenix, Arizona, but formerly of Seattle. They were married in British Columbia, Canada, and Elliott adopted her four children by a previous marriage, giving them the Roosevelt name.

In 1963, they moved to Miami, where he was a business consultant. In 1965, he was elected mayor of Miami Beach. Patty, whom he had met when she sold some property in Arizona for him, helped him campaign.

The couple live with their eight children in a large Spanish-style house on Biscayne Bay.

James Roosevelt, the President's eldest son who was married to Betsy Cushing at the time his father became President, was divorced by her on February 20, 1940, after ten years of marriage. She is now the wife of John Hay Whitney.

In April 1941, James married Romelle Schneider, 25, a brown-eyed nurse he met while undergoing treatment for a stomach ailment at a Rochester, Minnesota, hospital.

They were married in a civil ceremony at the home of Mr. and Mrs. George P. Converse in Beverly Hills. The First Lady flew to the West Coast to attend the ceremony, while Anna Boettiger and her husband flew down from Seattle.

The President and Mrs. Roosevelt gave the bride a diamond sapphire pin, and the First Lady gave her also a smaller gold pin that had belonged to her mother.

After the bridegroom returned from war service, the couple lived in California and had three children: James, Jr., now a sophomore at Harvard; Michael, a freshman at Harvard; and Anne, in college in California.

James has two children by his first wife: Sarah Delano, now Mrs. Anthony di Bonaventura of New York, and Kate, now Mrs. William Haddad, also of New York.

In 1954, James was elected to Congress from California. The following year, he was divorced by Romelle, and on July 2, 1956, he married Gladys Irene Owens, a secretary in his Washington office. It was a seven-minute ceremony at the home of a minister friend, the Rev. George Lyon Pratt in Los Angeles.

In September 1965, James resigned his seat in Congress to accept appointment as the United States Representative to the Economic and Social Council of the United Nations. He and Irene live in New York with an adopted son, Hall Delano.

XIX

More Roosevelt Era Weddings

Ethel duPont - Franklin D. Roosevelt, Jr.
June 30, 1937

Suzanne Perrin - Franklin D. Roosevelt, Jr.
August 31, 1949

Anne Lindsay Clark - John Roosevelt
June 18, 1938

Irene Boyd McAlpin - John Roosevelt
October 22, 1965

Louise Gill Macy - Harry Hopkins
July 30, 1942

icturesque Christ Episcopal Church at Christiana Hundred, Delaware, four miles from Wilmington, was the setting of the marriage on June 30, 1937, of President Franklin D. Roosevelt's third son and namesake, Franklin D., Jr., to Ethel duPont.

It was a brilliant society wedding attended by many members of the two famous families, who concealed their intense political enmity for the occasion. The anti-New Deal duPonts had opposed Roosevelt in two presidential campaigns and those family members unwilling to bury the political hatchet conveniently arranged to be abroad at the time of the wedding.

The President was warmly welcomed by the bride's father, Eugene duPont, when he arrived at the latter's home, the Owls Nest, following the ceremony.

Equally as cordial, the Chief Executive promised he would come back again and duPont asked that he wear his sailing whites the next time.

The wedding ceremony was performed by the 80-year-old Rev. Endicott Peabody. He had united the President and Mrs. Roosevelt in holy matrimony 32 years earlier at a wedding where another President, Theodore Roosevelt, had led the bride to the altar and was the ranking guest. The Rev. Mr. Peabody had also officiated at the marriage of Anna Roosevelt, their eldest child, to Curtis Dall in 1926.

Tiny Christ Church, the duPont family's place of worship since it was founded 78 years earlier by Colonel Henry duPont,

John Roosevelt and Anne Clark leave "Boston Church" in Nahant, Mass., following their wedding on June 18, 1938.

Wide World Photo

had been repainted inside and out for the five o'clock wedding. It was filled to capacity with the 392 guests.

The atmosphere was scented with some 2,000 sprays of Madagascar jasmine, which had been shipped across the country; the white waxy, star-shaped blossoms were scattered throughout the bouquets of peonies and lilies clustered on the ends of alternate pews on the center aisle.

For an hour before the ceremony, Dr. Charles M. Courboin, Belgian-born American artist, gave an organ concert. Five minutes before five, the President arrived. His train had pulled into Greenville shortly after noon and the Presidential party had gone to the home of Mr. and Mrs. Porter Schutt for luncheon.

Later they had returned to the train to dress for the wedding before setting out on the winding four-mile route to the church. The route was lined by 300 armed soldiers in crisp khaki and white gloves.

As the organ pealed out strains of the wedding march, the bridal party moved down the aisle. First came the ushers, dressed in continental cutaways with white double-breasted vests, white spats, turndown collars and gray ties. Next came the six bridesmaids in floating gowns of *mousseline de soie* over white taffeta to which natural sprays of maidenhair fern were fastened. Their soft wide-brimmed hats were trimmed with green or yellow streamers and wreaths of white violets.

Anna Roosevelt Boettiger, sister of the bridegroom, was matron of honor, and Aimee dePont was maid of honor.

The bride's costume was fashioned of white tulle lined with white crepe under a net clouding and set off with a 12-foot train, bordered with an inch-wide ruffle of the same material. The bouffant skirt had a narrow girdle of wax orange blossoms. The form-fitting bodice had three rows of shirring caught together in a V at the neckline with a clasp of wax orange blossoms. The sleeves were short and puffed, and there were matching elbow-length mittens. Her veil, fastened to a Juliet cap designed with miniature orange blossoms, was of white tulle and formed three layers, ten feet, six feet and three feet respectively, each edged with silver thread.

She carried a small prayer book of antique carved ivory to which were fastened sprays of dove orchids and a spray of stephanotis and lilies of the valley.

The prayer book, published by French printers in 1889, was "the something old" in the bride's ensemble. The something blue was the star sapphire bracelet set in a platinum backing made especially for her and a gift from the bridegroom. Her gift to him was an open-faced watch bearing the inscription "To F.D.R. from E. duP., June 30, 1937."

There was one blemish on the day. Just as the wedding party was leaving the church, a severe thunderstorm broke and rain whipped by a high wind drenched the bridesmaids' gowns and delayed the procession to Owls Nest, where a reception was held for the 392 wedding guests plus some 900 additional guests.

It was nine o'clock before the last car rolled into the grounds and already the toasts had been drunk. There were two. The first, by the President, was to the bride. The second, by the bridegroom, to whom the President handed his glass of champagne, was "to Mother."

Mrs. Roosevelt left the reception early to make her weekly broadcast from a station in Wilmington. The President made a joyous ceremony out of the traditional kissing of the bride and bridesmaids. As he kissed the bride, she clutched his lapels and reached up to whisper something in his ear. He threw back his head with a laugh. He had such a good time at the reception that he stayed 45 minutes longer than his original scheduled departure for Hyde Park.

Gifts to the bridal couple were lavish and numerous. The President and First Lady gave a large chest of flat silver; the Cabinet sent a nest of five silver service platters; the bride's mother gave an engraved silver tea and coffee service with large matching tray.

Two rooms and an upstairs hall were given over for the display of gifts and the silver gifts alone filled one room.

During the first three years of their married life the young couple lived in Charlottesville, Virginia, where young Roosevelt studied law at the University of Virginia. Their first child, Franklin D., III, was born on July 19, 1938. A second son, Christopher, was born December 22, 1941. Franklin D., III, now married and the father of three children, is a teacher at Columbia University. Christopher, also married, is a law student in Washington, D.C.

When Franklin D., Jr., entered politics in New York, the once-happy marriage began to break. Ethel did not care for politics nor the life of a politician's wife. She won a Nevada divorce in April 1949, one month before her husband was elected to Congress.

On August 31 of that year, Franklin married Suzanne Perrin, a slim blond New York socialite who had served in the Women's Marine Corps during World War II.

Theirs was a small, quiet wedding in the bride's apartment on East 66th Street in New York. Guests included the bridegroom's mother and her longtime secretary, Malvina Thompson. Elliott was his brother's best man this time. John had served as best man at the first wedding.

Suzanne met Franklin in Long Island social circles after he moved into a house near Westbury. She loved politics and has joined in his political interests and activities. The couple has two daughters, Nancy and Laura.

The second big wedding during the period the Roosevelts were in the White House came on June 18, 1938. This time the bridegroom was John, the youngest Roosevelt son, who had just graduated from Harvard. The bride was Anne Lindsay Clark, a petite blond Boston socialite.

The wedding was held in the historic century-old Union Church of Nahant, Massachusetts. It was as lavish as the Roosevelt-duPont nuptials a year earlier and nearly twice as large.

The 616 guests included scores of socially prominent families in Boston, New York, Delaware and Washington. So many spectators—about 5,000—turned out in the picturesque little resort town near Lynn that they blocked the path to the church. As a result, the bridegroom and his brother Franklin, who served as best man, had to jump a rope stretched to hold back the crowd to get to the church.

It was a noon wedding and as the hand-pumped organ pealed out the Lohengrin wedding march, the bridegroom and his best man walked down the aisle. Preceding the bride were 13 ushers, six bridesmaids, a matron of honor and a flower girl.

The bride's gown was fashioned of 20 yards of white French voile and trimmed with 630 yards of narrow satin-backed ribbon cleverly worked in an oak leaf design. On her head was a halo of imported orange blossoms and draped at the back was a sweeping train about 30 feet long. She wore a string of pearls that was a wedding gift from Mrs. Roosevelt.

Bishop Henry Knox Sherrill, head of the Episcopal Archdiocese in Boston, read the first part of the marriage ceremony, after which the Rev. Mr. Peabody took over the service. He had also officiated at the marriage of the bride's parents and at her christening service, as well as at the wedding of the groom's parents.

After the ceremony a reception was held in the Nahant Tennis Club. In the receiving line were the President, his mother, the bride's mother, the bride and bridegroom, the ushers and the bridesmaids.

The reception menu included cold whole salmon with mayonnaise, lettuce, tomato and cucumber salad, cold cuts, chicken a la king, fresh green peas, buttered rolls, vanilla ice cream with fresh strawberries, assorted cakes, demitasse, United Kingdom cuvee (champagne), and temperance punch.

To prepare the food for the more than 600 guests, the steward bought 300 pounds of chicken; five 12-pound turkeys, 90 pounds of ham, fifteen 12-pound Kennebec River salmon, two whole baby lambs for cold cuts, 14 bushels of green peas, 12 whole tongues, 25 pounds of potato chips, 40 gallons of ice cream, 300 boxes of strawberries, 70 dozen assorted cakes, 25 pounds of coffee, 50 pounds of lump sugar, five two-gallon cans of cream, 25 pounds butter, 80 dozen rolls, 12 gallons of temperance punch and 500 bottles of champagne.

One of the first to leave the reception was Mrs. Roosevelt, who motored to Hyde Park with her grandchildren, Eleanor and Curtis Dall.

The President who had traveled by train the previous night from Washington to Salem, Massachusetts, where he boarded the Presidential yacht *Potomac*, returned to the yacht and sailed on to Hyde Park to spend the weekend at his home there.

The bridal couple went first to the Roosevelt summer home at Campobello, and then spent six weeks on a European honeymoon. They returned in August to the $75,000 modernistic pink stucco "summer cottage" at Nahant, which was built as a wedding gift from the bride's mother.

John and Anne had four children: Haven Clark, who graduated from Yale Law School in 1966; Ann Sturgis (Nina) who is married to Douglas Luke, a graduate student at the Universtiy of Virginia; Sarah Delano (Sallie) who died a few years ago following a fall from a horse; and Joan, who lives with her mother but spends weekends with her father at Hyde Park.

This marriage lasted for nearly 28 years. On October 22, 1965, John, a senior vice-president and director of a Wall Street brokerage house, was granted a Mexican divorce on the grounds of incompatibility. Seven days later he married 33-year-old Irene Boyd McAlpin of Memphis and New York City, who was divorced earlier that year from her husband, also a Wall Street investment broker.

Their wedding took place at the Hampshire House, Manhattan home of the new Mrs. Roosevelt's parents. Anna Halsted, the bridegroom's sister, was the only member of his family attending.

The only marriage to take place in the White House during the Roosevelt Administration and the last one to be performed in the Executive Mansion was that of Harry Hopkins, President Roosevelt's top assistant, to Louise Gill Macy on July 30, 1942.

The President served as best man for Hopkins, who was his lend-lease expeditor during World War II and was then living in the White House.

The bride, a slim, smart-looking 36-year-old former Paris editor of *Harper's Bazaar*, had operated a dress shop in New York since her return from Paris at the beginning of the war.

It was a noon ceremony in the President's study that is now the oval drawing room in the First Family's private quarters on the second floor of the White House. The bride wore a street-length dress of deep blue crepe.

The wedding was attended only by members of the two families, the President and Mrs. Roosevelt and a few close friends. Hopkins' nine-year-old daughter, Diana, was there along with her three half-brothers. There was no music during the ceremony but a Meyer Davis Orchestra played during the breakfast which followed.

After a brief wedding trip the couple and Diana lived at the White House in the suite occupied by Hopkins before the marriage.

Hopkins died in January 1946 and his widow was married again in September 1947 to Geoffrey Gates, director of the

Parsons School of Design in New York. She died three years ago.

Diana Hopkins is married to Allin Baxter, a lawyer, and lives in Washington. They have two children. She often tells them about the days when she lived in the White House.

Recently Audrey, her daughter, was taken by her nurse on one of the public tours of the State Rooms of the White House. She ran out of the line of visitors to a window and clutching a curtain looked out onto the lawn. When a guard asked her to return to the line, she saucily turned her head and to his surprise said "My mommy used to live here." And indeed she had.

Mr. and Mrs. Harry Hopkins, center, at their wedding in the President's oval study on second floor of the White House. President Franklin Delano Roosevelt, seated, served as best man to his top assistant. Mrs. Roosevelt is second from Hopkins on the right.

XX

The 1966
White House
Bride

Luci Baines Johnson - Patrick John Nugent
August 6, 1966

uci Baines Johnson, the 1966 White House Bride, was the eighth Presidential daughter to be married while living in the Executive Mansion. Her wedding on August 6, 1966, to 23-year-old Patrick John Nugent was a young girl's dream come true. Luci, the younger daughter of President and Mrs. Lyndon B. Johnson, was both romantic and religious and her wedding shattered old precedents and set new ones.

She was the first Presidential daughter to be married in a church.

She was the first Presidential daughter to be married in a Catholic ceremony.

She was the first bride to be married in the National Shrine of the Immaculate Conception, the largest Catholic Church in the United States.

And she was married in a religious ceremony that incorporated many recent liturgical changes, including the serving of bread and wine rather than bread alone to the bride and bridegroom, as is customary for Catholic laity.

After being married in one of the most beautiful and brilliant weddings Washington had seen in many decades, she went flying off to honeymoon in a secluded seaside villa in the Bahamas loaned by the millionairess Rebekah Harkness Kean.

Luci's wedding was a little larger than she had ever dreamed, although the White House described it from the beginning as a "private family affair" rather than a state occasion. There were more than 700 guests. Most were close personal and family friends, with the very top layer of Washington officials added—cabinet officers, Supreme Court Justices, a dozen members of

Mr. and Mrs. Patrick John Nugent leave the National Shrine of the Immaculate Conception following their marriage on August 6, 1966.

Washington Post Photo by Vic Casamento

Congress and the dean of the Diplomatic Corps, Nicaraguan Ambassador Guillermo Sevilla Sacasa.

The Right Reverend Patrick A. O'Boyle, Archbishop of Washington, celebrated the nuptial Mass. It was he also who granted special permission for Luci to be married in the Shrine. The marriage ceremony was performed by the Reverend John Kuzinskas, of Waukegan, Illinois, a life-long friend of the bridegroom. And in the concelebrated Mass, the Reverend William J. Kaifer, S.J., who was Luci's spiritual adviser at the Georgetown University School of Nursing, read the Gospel.

Instead of a soloist, a 150-voice men and boys' choir from two Catholic churches in Baltimore sang. The wedding music was played on a $250,000 pipe organ considered one of the greatest in the western world.

Luci had her closest friends as bridesmaids; there were ten of them, more than had attended any other White House bride. In addition, Luci had a maid of honor, her sister, Lynda Bird, plus a matron of honor and a flower girl.

It was a wedding marked with great beauty and deep religious significance, and the logistics were so carefully planned that everything went off with clocklike precision.

Luci had met Patrick Nugent at a surprise party on the evening of June 1, 1965. That was the day she graduated from National Cathedral School for Girls. This was one month before her 18th birthday.

Her sister, Lynda, and some of Luci's friends planned the surprise party, held in the White House third-floor solarium. The night before they had telephoned Luci's childhood friend, Beth Jenkins, a student at Marquette University, and asked her to come. Beth and four friends—a girl and three boys—drove all night from Wisconsin to Washington for the party. The extra boy was Patrick Nugent, a tall, handsome blond from Waukegan, Illinois, who was to graduate a week later from Marquette University.

Vivacious, brunette, blue-eyed Luci did not pay too much attention to Patrick that evening. He was quiet and reserved and besides she had difficulty understanding his midwestern accent. But when the Marquette five started to leave, Luci wistfully said, "I wish I could do something wild and crazy like you all."

"Come to Marquette for the senior prom next weekend," Beth invited.

Turning to Patrick, Beth asked, "Do you have a date?"

He said, "No."

"You do now, it's with Luci," Beth said, and it was thus arranged.

That was a weekend to remember. Luci wore a silver blond wig in order to conceal her identity. She used another name, Amy Nunn, and went where she pleased without being recognized.

That weekend stretched into a summer romance that ripened into love after young Nugent came to Washington the following month.

He called Luci at the White House and was one of the small group at St. Matthew's Cathedral on July 2 when Luci was baptized into the Catholic church. He was with her when she made her first Roman Catholic communion. But so was Paul Betz, a young pre-medical student whose fraternity pin Luci had returned just before she met Pat.

Luci had been baptized into the Episcopal Church when she was 13 but some time later became a practicing Catholic. At her parents' request she waited until she was 18 to follow her new faith into baptism.

The fact that she was baptized a second time, which some clergymen felt was unnecessary, caused considerable discussion in pulpits and in the press across the country. Luci found herself in the middle of a religious debate over the manner of her entry into the Catholic church.

Pat, a deeply religious Catholic, felt sorry for her and said he would not leave her alone in Washington while the controversy continued. (Luci's parents had left the White House shortly after the baptism to spend the long holiday weekend at the LBJ ranch in Texas). Pat found himself an apartment and a job in Washington and stood by her as she carried on in her new faith.

That summer he was a frequent luncheon guest at the White House and made a splendid impression on Luci's parents and her friends. The two had many dates, which Luci somehow managed to conceal from the public and the press. They went together to the New York World's Fair; they made trips to

Camp David, Maryland, the Presidential mountain retreat, and to the LBJ ranch near Johnson City, Texas.

Luci visited his family, Mr. and Mrs. Gerard Nugent, at their modest brick-veneer bungalow on Prescott Street, in Waukegan. And she attended the wedding of Pat's older brother, Gerard Jr. (Jerry) on August 7, 1965.

By this time Pat and Luci were very much in love.

In September Luci entered Georgetown University School of Nursing as a freshman. Pat settled into his job as administrative assistant to the chairman of the District of Columbia Advisory Commission on Higher Education until he entered the Air National Guard in November 1965.

Quiet and reserved, Pat was much more at ease with small groups than a big crowd. But his soft voice, gentle manners and poise in meeting the many important people who came to the White House impressed the President and First Lady. Pat had grown up in a Lithuanian working-class neighborhood where his father, in the insurance and investments business, had an office on the enclosed front porch of their bungalow. His parents had given him every educational opportunity, as well as the security and love of a good home.

He went to kindergarten and elementary school at St. Bartholomew's in Waukegan, and to Campion High School, an expensive Jesuit boarding school in Prairie du Chien, Wisconsin. At Marquette University, where he took his degree in history, he was a popular student who dated the best-looking girls on the campus and became a fraternity and campus leader.

He had planned to go to law school, but after his military service and his engagement to Luci, he changed his plans and decided to get a master's degree in business administration. He enrolled in night college courses and often studied in the evenings at the White House with Luci.

Like so many children of Congressmen, Luci's childhood was divided between home (Texas) and Washington. She attended Cassis Elementary School in Austin half of the year and Ben Murch in Washington the other half until she entered the eighth grade at National Cathedral School the year her father was elected Vice-President.

Shortly after she became a teenager, she changed the spelling of her name from Lucy to Luci.

Luci Johnson Nugent and her husband, Patrick John, stand on the South Portico of the White House while members of the wedding party descend the steps. The bridesmaids wore gowns of pink moire.

At 13 she began having dates. Before she met Pat, she had a string of boy friends. Some gave her their class rings, which she wore with big wads of adhesive tape on the inside to make them fit her tiny finger; others gave her their fraternity pins to wear.

Most of them remained good friends after she started going steady with young Nugent. But Luci never let her dating interfer with what she regarded as her "duties" as the daughter of a President. Though she considered herself the "unpolitical member of a political family," in the 1964 Presidential campaign, she spent her weekends flying to various cities to speak and shake hands at LBJ barbecues in behalf of the Democratic ticket. At the White House she served as substitute hostess for her mother on numerous occasions and extended impromptu greetings to groups calling on her father. She served as honorary chairman of the United Cerebral Palsy "Tag Day" and as honorary chairman of the National Symphony Orchestra's series of concerts for young people. She was a very active member of Volunteers for Vision, a group which assisted in administering tests to detect eye defects among pre-schoolers in the anti-poverty program.

Two summers she also worked part-time as an assistant in the office of an optometrist.

She never quite relished living in the White House, however. "You feel so alone, the ceilings are so high. It's kind of morbid walking down the halls and never meeting anyone," she once said. But she was grateful for the experience of living there.

"It's a wonderful experience and education because I can watch history in the making. I have been able to talk with world leaders," she said.

Luci chose her own niche in the 166-year-old mansion. It was the third-floor solarium with its tan tile floor, comfortable chairs and sofas dotted with plump pillows, the soft-drink machine, record player, and after she moved in, the cluttered, lived-in look of a teenager's room. Here she entertained her friends at luncheons and at small dinners she herself cooked. Here she and Pat often studied together; it was one place they were not under the watchful eyes of the Secret Service.

On the first Friday in October, Pat proposed to Luci in church. He asked her twice more before she gave him a definite

yes. The next hurdle was winning her father's consent to their marriage. Luci didn't have to tell her mother their romance had reached the stage of talking marriage. "Mothers and daughters are always so close that mothers can sense those things," Luci said.

But before Pat got around to speaking to her father about it, newspapers had published the fact that they wanted to be married.

About three weeks later her father asked in a very jovial mood, "What is all this stuff I have been reading in the papers?" Pat had his lines memorized and recited them. The President said, "Well, let's sit down and discuss the pros and cons."

"We found something on each side of the situation," Luci related later. And the President ended by saying "Well, I want what you want to make you happy. I trust your judgment and I approve. Why don't we talk about it some more?" And they did, at a later date.

On Christmas eve, Pat gave Luci the ring he had designed for her. It had a one-carat diamond in the center flanked by a one-half carat diamond on each side. She wore it to midnight Mass while Elizabeth Carpenter, press secretary to the First Lady, was telephoning newspapers to give them the announcement of their engagement.

Luci and Pat spent Christmas day with her parents and flew that afternoon to Waukegan to be with his parents. She wore a glowing smile that matched the sparkle of her new ring. No date was set for the wedding then. That came on Valentine's Day, after Mr. and Mrs. Nugent made their first visit to the White House to meet the parents of their future daughter-in-law.

The date was set for August 6 and the place chosen was the National Shrine of the Immaculate Conception. Wedding plans began to unfold on a schedule worked out by Mrs. Carpenter and other members of the First Lady's staff.

Patrick served his basic training in the Air National Guard at Lackland Air Force Base in San Antonio, Texas, and was assigned to Andrews Air Force Base near Washington. This enabled him to see Luci and also to enroll at American University for evening courses preparatory to work toward a master's degree in business administration. When he finished his military

185

training, he returned to his job with the Advisory Commission on Higher Education.

On May 1, Luci's bridesmaids and Patrick's attendants were announced. She chose as her maid of honor her sister, Lynda Bird Johnson, who graduated in June from the University of Texas, and as matron of honor, Mrs. James Ray of Hale Center, Texas, whom Luci had met three years earlier while her husband was working in Washington as administrative assistant to Representative George Mahon of Texas.

Some of Luci's bridesmaids had gone to school with her, others shared double dates and parties, barbecues and window shopping. They were Betty Beal, Austin, Texas; Kathleen Carter, Arlington, Virginia; Sharon Chapman, Arlington, Virginia; Mrs. Gerard Nugent, Jr., San Diego, California; Beth Jenkins, Austin, Texas; Helene Lindow, Washington, D.C.; Patti McGouirk, Fort Worth, Texas; Mrs. James Montelaro, Washington, D.C.; Charlotte Sizoo, Arlington, Virginia; and Warrie Lynn Smith, San Antonio, Texas.

Patrick picked as his best man his brother, Marine Lieutenant Gerard Nugent, Jr., but since he was serving in Vietnam, he asked his father, Gerard P. Nugent to serve as proxy for the brother. He chose as his groomsmen friends from boyhood days, roommates and friends from boarding school and college, plus several cousins and friends met through Luci. They were Larry Carr, Waukegan, Illinois; William A. Ganz, Mascoutah, Illinois; Michael Gronniger, Waukegan, Illinois; James D. Hall, Waukegan, Illinois; William B. Hitchcock, III, Austin, Texas; Loren Leskis, Waukegan, Illinois; Dr. Bernard McQuillan, Hazelwood, Missouri; Timothy Matelenas, Waukegan, Illinois; James Montelaro, Washington, D.C.; Joseph M. Ness, Wayzata, Minnesota; and Bruce Pecaro, Waukegan, Illinois.

Also in the wedding party were two 5-year-old attendants: Lyndon "Corky" Hand, son of Mr. and Mrs. Lloyd Hand of Los Angeles, California, who was ring bearer; and Bader Howar, daughter of Mr. and Mrs. Edmond Howar of Washington, D.C., flower girl.

Early in July the coveted invitations to the wedding were mailed to some 700 "personal friends and relatives" of the bride and groom and their families. The invitation was on ecru paper

*These are the mementos Luci Johnson Nugent carried during her wedding.
The something old is the 58-year-old ivory lace handkerchief made by her
great-grandmother, Ruth Ament Huffman. The rosary given to Lynda Bird
Johnson by Pope John XXIII, is the something borrowed. The something
blue is the gold locket tied with a blue satin ribbon belonging to Mrs.
Gerard Nugent, mother. of the bridegroom. The pictures in the locket are
Mrs. Nugent's two sons during childhood. The sixpence is one of several
sent to Luci by people across the country. She wore it in her shoe.*

engraved in hand-cut script with the Presidential coat-of-arms
embossed at the center top.

On July 18, Luci did something no other White House
Bride before her had done. She invited some 80 reporters who
write regularly about the activities of the First Family to a tea
party in the State Dining Room for a final chat and farewell.
She sat beside her mother on a sofa in front of the fireplace
and answered questions about her courtship, romance and plans
for the future. The first question was where she would live.

She described the $165-a-month brick duplex on Heritage
Way in Austin which she and Patrick had rented as their first
home. It had five rooms: a living room, two bedrooms, a kitchen
with a copper-colored stove, a dinette area, a hallway and two
skylights which, she said, "I find just great . . . they save
electricity."

Luci said she and Pat both would attend the University of
Texas, Pat working on a master's degree in business administration and she working on an undergraduate degree.

Asked why they chose Texas, she said: "It is home for me
and I love it. Patrick has come to love it in the same way that
I do . . . I feel I will be able to get a little more privacy at
home . . . I think it is a good starting-off place for young people
in my situation."

When she was asked if it was love at first sight when she
met Pat and what characteristics attracted her to him, Luci
smiled.

"No, I wouldn't say that it was love at first sight," she
said. "I would say it was a thing that grew because of mutual
interests and because of the kind of individual that Patrick is."

"What attracted me to him—a thousand things," she continued. "You would have to describe Patrick to say what
attracted me to him. He is a very honest person, a very sincere
person, a very sincerely religious person, which attracts me to
him a great deal, because as far as we are both concerned, our
marriage can only survive and grow through our religion. Because we feel the same way about our religion, we feel that we
will grow closer together and appreciate more in life as a result
of that common bond."

Her deeply religious feeling was reflected in the wedding
band she gave Patrick on their wedding day. It was a plain

gold band engraved inside "Together Through Christ. L.J. to P.N. 8-6-66."

During the month preceding her wedding, there was a party for Luci almost every other day. The Cabinet wives gave a luncheon in her honor at the home of Mrs. Robert S. McNamara, wife of the Secretary of Defense; Associate Justice and Mrs. Tom Clark gave a party honoring Luci and Pat in the stately, marble Supreme Court; Ambassador-at-large and Mrs. Averell Harriman gave a reception at their Georgetown house for the couple and invited members of the Diplomatic Corps to meet them. There were many other dinners, luncheons, teas and showers which kept Luci and her friends on the go.

President Johnson was obviously pleased with his future son-in-law, but it was not until the eve of the wedding that he publicly expressed his feelings. At the rehearsal dinner given by the groom's parents at the George Town Club, the President said in a toast: "Every father worries about the man his daughter marries. But I want to say that I stopped being nervous when I met Pat. He makes me very proud of Luci because you can tell a lot about a girl by the kind of man she likes."

Earlier the President told reporters that he had always wanted a son and was getting in Pat the kind of boy he wanted. "You're struck at once by his politeness, he's so logical, knows his own mind and Luci looks up to him with great respect, deep affection and confidence in him . . . it's going to be a good marriage."

Before the wedding at twelve o'clock noon on Saturday, some members of the White House staff worked all night decorating the mansion and the Shrine for the events. The huge Shrine, which is marked by unusual beauty, looked almost like a formal garden. White flowers and great masses of greenery were used throughout in restrained elegance. Every fourth pew had markers of greens, ivy and white flowers—roses, babies breath, album lilies, and white delphinium. Miniature markers of the same flowers and greens were used on the kneelers for the bridal party in the chancel.

Willowy greenery—locust and ficus trees—were used throughout the Shrine. These were decorated with white roses, lily-of-the valley and babies breath. The trees surrounding the altar were topiary in shape. Two tall silver vases on each side of the altar held white delphiniums, album lilies and other mixed white flowers. The fragrance of the flowers perfumed the church. Ropes of green smilax marked off the pews that were not used for seating the guests. Although only about 700 were invited, the church could comfortably seat 3,500 guests.

At the White House, where the reception was held, a white canopy was placed over the Jacqueline Kennedy Garden where the wedding reception guests assembled before going up to the Blue Room to greet the bridal couple and their parents. The tent had a pink lining and the poles and ropes were decorated with pink and white carnations and greens.

The long corridor through which the guests walked to the Blue Room was lined with green buckets of white petunias and pink geraniums. The gold chandelier in the State Dining Room was used as a holder from which greens and flowers cascaded, and compotes of yellow, white, blue and orange flowers decorated the buffet table in the State Dining Room.

Swags of greens highlighted with flowers festooned the four columns in the entrance hall on the State floor and the gold torcherers in the hall were decorated with greens and flowers. Red roses and rubrum lilies, accented by pink and white flowers, highlighted the historic Red Room, while green Nicotiana, lavender and pink and white flowers decorated the Green Room. Arrangements of white, yellow, red and blue flowers decorated the East Room where the buffet table was covered with an off-white tablecloth.

The White House was bustling with activity early on the day of the wedding. Jean Louis, the French hair stylist who had the day before arranged hair styles for the bride, her mother and sister, nearly all her bridesmaids and the groom's mother, set up shop at seven o'clock that morning in the East Hall on the second floor of the Executive Mansion. One by one he gave each a fresh comb-out and styling.

The bride arose at eight and spent the morning preparing for the wedding, interrupted frequently by bridesmaids, who were staying at the White House, dropping in for conversation.

The historic Lincoln bedroom was used as a bridal dressing room, and Luci's gown, stuffed with paper, was hung in the closet. Spread across the seven-foot bed was her veil and train, and against one wall was a rack of bridesmaids' dresses, all designed by Priscilla (Mrs. James Kidder) of Boston.

Luci chose a bridal gown she could hand down to her grandchildren. It was designed of white rosepoint Alencon appliques lightly embroidered with seed pearls. The neckline was a wedding band shape of lace scalloped and outlined with seed pearls. The sleeves were long and tapered, touched with pearls on the edge and small buttons up the side. The high Empire bodice was outlined in scalloped lace as was the semi-molded skirt, which had a slight flare in the back.

The cathedral—three-yard—train of matching lace was edged with scallops and encrusted with pearls. It was attached below the shoulders to a little lace casque at the back and caught with a peau-de-soie bow. Tiny buttons accented the back dress line under the Watteau paneled train. Under the Alencon lace gown was a peau-de-soie underdress. Embroidered in blue on the hemline of this dress was her name and her wedding date.

Luci wore a starched illusion veil shaped into a pouff-capote gathered in the back with matching lace and pearl appliques. The crown of the shoulder length veil was Alencon appliqued also. She wore white satin shoes with a one-inch shaped heel and at the front of the shoe, a white satin rose.

Her attendants' gowns were a blending of August pinks. The ten bridesmaids wore bright "pink-pink" gowns of moire, with a rolled wedding ring neckline to match the edges of the sleeves and the floor-length hemline. The bodice was a molded silhouette easing into a stemline-shaped skirt flowing slightly in the back. Buttons of a matching fabric trimmed the back. Floor-length illusion veils worn at the back of the head were of contrasting pink. The maid of honor and matron of honor wore gowns of the same design in pale, frosted pink with illusion veils of shaded hues of pink.

With their gowns the attendants wore wrist-length white kid gloves and shoes of a fabric to match the gowns. Their nosegays were a blend of pink roses, lilies-of-the-valley and illusion. The bride's bouquet was of white lilies-of-the-valley in an arrangement eight inches across.

In selecting the gowns, Luci, who had originally chosen blue for her attendants, had the assistance of Stanley Marcus, a lifelong friend and the president of Neiman Marcus of Dallas, where the gowns were purchased.

The bridegroom's attendants wore traditional wedding morning suits—Oxford grey cutaway coats with pearl grey single-breasted vests and striped trousers.

At eleven o'clock guests began arriving at the Shrine for the noon wedding. It was a bright, sunny day with the temperature in the low eighties. More than 200 photographers and reporters for newspapers, magazines, radio and television lined the 36 steps leading to the Shrine entrance to watch the parade into the church. About eleven-thirty the bridegroom and his father arrived, the former admitting to reporters he was a little nervous. The groom and his attendants had dressed in the President's Guest House across the street from the White House.

Some ten minutes later Luci arrived with her mother and father, the latter wearing the formal morning outfit with cutaway coat that he had spurned at his own inauguration as President. Mrs. Johnson wore a short dress and coat ensemble of lemon sherbet silk crystalline with Peau d'Ange lace molded over the dress and coat. It was designed by Adele Simpson. With the ensemble she wore yellow shoes, a yellow silk turban and carried a roll bag of matching yellow silk.

Luci, who looked lovely with her blue eyes glistening in the sun and her dark hair beautifully coiffed under her veil, kept an old bridal tradition by wearing "something old, something new, something borrowed and something blue and a sixpence in your shoe."

Her something old was a 58-year-old ivory lace handkerchief made by her paternal great-grandmother, Ruth Ament Huffman. Her wedding dress was the something new. The something borrowed was a rosary of mother-of-pearl and gold given to her sister by Pope John XXIII during a family audience on September 7, 1962. As something blue, she carried a gold locket tied with a blue satin ribbon belonging to the mother of the groom. It was given to Mrs. Nugent by her mother when her two sons where young and contains childhood pictures of the two boys. The sixpence Luci carried was one of several sent to her by people across the country, this one a gift from Adele Roscoe of Perth Amboy, New Jersey.

For one hour before the ceremony the famous 56-bell carillon in the slender golden-spired Knights Tower, which rises 329 feet above the Shrine, pealed and played with carillonneur Robert Grogan at the massive keyboard.

The carillon program included:

Preludio IX in F Major	Van den Gheyn
Andante (Concerto I in G for Organ)	Handel
"O let the merry bells ring 'round" (from "L'Allegro")	Handel
Partita I for Carillon	Franco

    Prelude
    Aria
    Toccata

Prelude (from Prelude, Fugue and Allegro for Lute)	Bach
Siciliano (Sonata I for Solo Violin)	Bach
Trumpet Tune and Air	Purcell
Two Chorale Preludes	Walther

    "Praise to the Lord, the Almighty, the King of Creation"
    "To God On High Be Glory"

Sinfonia (from "Solomon")	Handel
The Angelus (Scenes Pittoresques)	Massenet

Three Lute Pieces of the Italian Renaissance

Galliard	Galilei
Danza	anon
Galliard	anon
The "St. Anthony" Chorale	Haydn
Prelude (Suite IV for Solo Cello)	Bach
"O nata lux de lumine"	Tallis
Pronunciamento for Carillon (1966) (first performance)	Franco

Inside the Shrine for 30 minutes prior to the ceremony, a program of organ music and selections by the combined choir from the Cathedral of Mary Our Queen and the Church of the Immaculate Heart of Mary in Baltimore were presented. Robert F. Twynham, who had played the dedicatory recital on the magnificent organ two years earlier, was in charge of the wedding music, and the choirs were under the direction of Norman Sydnor of Baltimore.

At the request of the bride, one Episcopal hymn was sung by the choir. It was "King's Weston" by Ralph Vaughn Williams, beginning with the stanza:

    "At the name of Jesus every knee shall bow,
    Every tongue confess him, King of Glory now.

'Tis the Father's pleasure we should call him Lord,
Who from the beginning was the mighty Word."

The organ program before the wedding ceremony included:

Sinfonia (Cantata 29) .... Bach
Jesu, Joy of Man's Desiring (choir) .... Bach
Scherzo (From Symphony II) .... Vierne
Jesu, Grant Me This I Pray (choir) ....Whitlock
Benedictus es, Domine.. Sowerby
"King's Weston" (choir)...Vaughn Williams
Chant de Pais .... Langlais
Wachet auf ruft uns die Stimme .... Bach
Prelude in G Minor.. Dupre
Psalm 150 (choir) .... Franck

There was stillness in the Shrine, fragrant with flowers, as
the bridal procession began at seven minutes after twelve o'clock.

As the great pipe organ boomed out Robert Twynham's
"Paraphrase on a Trumpet Tune by Henry Purcell," the procession moved up the 352-foot aisle. First were the groomsmen,
followed by the bridegroom and his father. Patrick wore a sprig
of lily-of-the-valley in his buttonhole. The attendants wore
white roses.

Behind them came the bridesmaids single file with Lynda
Bird last. Following close behind was the ringbearer, Lyndon
"Corky" Hand, dressed in white, and then trailing far behind
was Bader Howar, the flower girl, also in white. She carried a
basket of roses but strewed no petals. Then came the President
and Luci.

While Luci looked from side to side nodding to friends, the
President, wearing a pleased and proud expression, kept his
eyes on the end of the aisle where waited the young man soon
to be his son-in-law.

Only once did he nod to a wedding guest and that was to
Vice-President Hubert H. Humphrey, who sat on the aisle in a
pew immediately behind the area reserved for the bride's family.

At the communion rail the President relinquished his daughter to the bridegroom. She slipped her left arm up on her
father's shoulder in an affectionate gesture as Pat slipped her
right hand through the crook of his left elbow and led her up
the chancel steps to the white satin covered *prie-dieu* where
they both knelt.

The lay reading was given by Representative Hale Boggs of Louisiana, a long-time friend of the bride and her family. He read from the Epistle of Paul the Apostle to the Ephesians: (Chapter 5, verses 22 through 33) which begins:

"Wives should be submissive to their husbands as though to the Lord; because the husband is head of the wife just as Christ is head of the Church, his body, of which He is also the Savior. Just as the Church submits to Christ, so should wives submit in everything to their husbands. Husbands, love your wives, just as Christ loved the Church and gave Himself up for her . . ."

The Reverend William J. Kaifer read the Gospel (Matthew 19: 3-5).

The crosses at the tips of Pat and Luci's rosaries glittered in the candlelight as the Reverend John Kuzinskas began the ten-minute marriage ritual. Luci was shaking slightly but kept her chin up and her eyes on the brilliant mosaic of Christ behind the altar. Pat reached for a handkerchief and wiped his eyes.

At the point in the exhortation where Father Kuzinskas said, "This union is most serious because it will bind you together for life in a relationship so close and so intimate that it will profoundly influence your whole future," Luci and Pat looked at each other. When he read, "That future with the hopes and disappointments, its successes and its failures," there was another exchange of looks as if to say we can take it, and tears welled in both their eyes as the priest continued:

"We are willing to give in proportion as we love and when love is perfect the sacrifice is complete."

Luci's voice was barely audible in the congregation as she said "I do," and Pat's response was too low to hear.

After the vows were sealed, the priest sprinkled holy water on the couple saying "What God has joined together, let no man put asunder."

It was a three-ring ceremony; Luci gave Pat a plain gold band and he gave her two diamond wedding bands to wear one on each side of her engagement ring. In blessing the rings, Father Kuzinskas departed from the ceremony in the printed missal given each wedding guest, asking the couple to say instead, "With this ring, I marry you and pledge to you my ever faithful love."

At 12:42 Father Kuzinskas pronounced, "I join you in sacred wedlock," and the ceremony was over. Pat and Luci turned and faced the congregation as husband and wife.

Archbishop O'Boyle, who celebrated the Mass, served the communion to the bridal couple. As they took the wine, the couple seemed unaware of the activity going on directly behind them. Priests were running to and fro bringing first smelling salts and then a chair for Lynda Bird, who had apparently felt faint, dropped her head and slumped over the kneeler. She was helped into the chair and remained seated for the remainder of the Mass.

At the conclusion of the Mass, Archbishop O'Boyle read a cablegram from the Vatican in which Pope Paul VI bestowed his personal blessings on the bridal couple, whom he had met when he was in New York to address the United Nations the preceding October. Signed by the Vatican Secretary of State Amleto Cardinal Cigognani, the message read in part: "On the joyous occasion of the wedding, the Holy Father bestows upon Patrick J. Nugent and Luci Johnson personal blessings and apostolic benediction and prays for abundant heavenly favor in their married life."

The bride, who had been a nursing student, took an extra bouquet to the Shrine Chapel of Our Lady of Mt. Carmel and left it before a picture of St. Agatha, the patron saint of nursing. On her way back to the aisle she paused to kiss first her mother, then her father, and then she stepped across the aisle and kissed the mother of her husband. Pat did likewise. Both had tears in their eyes.

On the way out of the church, they paused and Pat shook hands with Senate Minority Leader Everett Dirksen of Illinois and Luci kissed him. Outside Luci and Pat got into a bubble-top limousine and looked back to wave to the bridal party that had followed them out of the church. As they rounded the curve leaving the Shrine, Pat leaned over and kissed his wife for the first time since their marriage.

Before the 700 wedding guests arrived at the White House for the reception, the bridal party posed for pictures and then the newlyweds joined their parents in the Blue Room to receive the guests. There were many hugs and kisses as congratulations and good wishes were extended. One of the guests was 82-year-old Alice Roosevelt Longworth, who had been married in the White House in 1906. Then Luci, with a lot of help from her husband and father, cut the 14-tiered wedding cake in the East Room. She used a sword-like knife that was a wedding gift from Senator and Mrs. Birch Bayh of Indiana.

It was a summer fruit cake baked by Ferdinand Louvat, French pastry chef at the White House, and there were seven layers with a tier of sugar arches framing sugar lilies-of-the-valley between each layer of cake. On top was a bride's cake, a chocolate cake, which the couple took on their honeymoon. On top of the cake were real lilies-of-the-valley in lieu of the traditional bells or miniature bride and groom.

The White House released a recipe for the fruit cake.

LUCI'S WEDDING CAKE

Cover ½ cup white seedless raisins with apple juice, and let soak in refrigerator 2 or 3 days (or until raisins are plump). Drain and spread on towel to dry surface moisture.

> 1¾ cups sifted cake flour
> 1 teaspoon double acting baking powder
> ¼ teaspoon salt
> ½ cup butter
> ¾ cup sugar
> 5 egg whites, unbeaten
> ¾ cup chopped candied pineapple
> 1 cup chopped pecans
> ½ cup soaked raisins
> ½ teaspoon almond extract
> ½ teaspoon vanilla extract

Sift flour once and measure. Add baking powder and salt and sift together three times. Cream butter thoroughly and add sugar gradually, creaming together until light and fluffy. Add egg whites, one at a time, beating thoroughly after each. Add fruit, nuts and flavoring and mix well. Add flour, a little at a time, beating after each addition until smooth. Bake in a loaf pan which has been greased, lined with heavy paper and greased again. Bake in a slow oven (300⁰) about one hour and 15 minutes or until done. For loaf cake, use pan 8 x 4 x 3, which serves 8-10 persons.

After the cake-cutting ceremony and a period of dancing to the music of Peter Duchin's orchestra, Luci and Pat went upstairs to change into travel clothes. Luci's ensemble was shocking pink with a pink and white silk turban. She and Pat went onto the South Balcony. From there Luci tossed her bride's bouquet to the attendants standing below. It was caught by her sister. Watching nearby was actor George Hamilton, Lynda Bird's beau, who had come from Hollywood for the wedding festivities.

Luci hugged and kissed her mother and father, then leaned over the balcony rail and said goodbye to her attendants, calling each of them by name. Then she looked out to the crowd on the lawn and said, "And I want to say goodbye to everybody else. It's been a beautiful, wonderful day. The most magnificent day of our lives." And they were off, making a secret getaway to a secret honeymoon hideaway.

The 1906 White House Bride, Alice Roosevelt Longworth, third from left, poses with the 1966 White House Bride, Luci Johnson Nugent, at the reception in the White House following the latter's wedding on August 7, 1966. In the receiving line are, from left, President Johnson, Luci, Mrs. Longworth, Patrick John Nugent, Mrs. Gerard Nugent, Mrs. Johnson, and Mr. Nugent.

Bibliography

Adams, Charles Francis, *The Diary of Charles Francis Adams*. Aida and David Donald, editors. Vols. 1 and 2. Cambridge, Mass.: The Belknap Press of Harvard University Press, copyright 1964 *Massachusetts Historical Society.*

Adams Papers, microfilm edition. Quotations from the diaries and letters of John Quincy Adams, Louisa Catherine Adams and George Washington Adams from the Adams Papers are from the microfilm edition, and are reprinted by permission of the *Massachusetts Historical Society.*

Alexander, Holmes, *The American Talleyrand.* New York and London: Harper & Brothers, Publishers, 1935.

Beale, Marie, *Decatur House and Its Inhabitants.* Washington: National Trust for Historic Preservation, 1954.

Bemis, Samuel Flagg, *John Quincy Adams and the Foundations of American Foreign Policy.* New York: Alfred A. Knopf, 1956.

Bemis, Samuel Flagg, *John Quincy Adams and the Union.* New York: Alfred A. Knopf, 1956.

Bobbé, Dorothie, *Mr. and Mrs. John Quincy Adams: An Adventure in Patriotism.* New York: Minton, Balch & Co., 1930.

Briggs, Emily E., *The Olivia Letters.* New York and Washington: The Neale Publishing Co., 1906.

Butt, Archibald W., *The Letters of Archie Butt.* Edited by Lawrence F. Abbott. Garden City, N.Y.: Doubleday, Page & Co., 1924.

Butt, Archibald W., *Taft and Roosevelt: The Intimate Letters of Archie Butt.* Garden City, N.Y.: Doubleday, Doran & Co., Inc., 1930.

Chitwood, Oliver Perry, *John Tyler, Champion of the Old South.* New York: Russell & Russell, Inc., 1964.

Clark, Allen C., *Life and Letters of Dolly Madison.* Washington, D.C.: W. F. Roberts Company, 1914.

Coleman, Elizabeth Tyler, *Priscilla Cooper Tyler and the American Scene.* University, Ala.: University of Alabama Press, 1955.

Coleman, Mary Haldane (Mrs. George P.), *St. George Tucker, Citizen of No Mean City.* Richmond, Virginia: The Dietz Press, 1938.

Coles, Strickler, *The Coles Family of Virginia.* New York: Copyright by Strickler Coles, 1931.

Colman, Edna M., *Seventy-five Years of White House Gossip; from Washington to Lincoln.* Garden City, N.Y.: Doubleday, Page & Co., 1926.

Colman, Edna M., *White House Gossip, from Andrew Johnson to Calvin Coolidge.* Garden City, N.Y.: Doubleday, Page & Co., 1927.

Cresson, William Penn, *James Monroe.* Chapel Hill: The University of North Carolina Press, 1946.

Crook, William H., *Memories of the White House.* Compiled and edited by Henry Rood. Boston: Little, Brown & Co., 1911.

Cutts, Lucia B., editor, *Memoirs and Letters of Dolly Madison.* Boston and New York: Houghton Mifflin Co., 1886.

Ervin, Janet Halliday, *The White House Cookbook.* Chicago: Follett Publishing Company, 1964.

Farrar, Emmie Ferguson, *Old Virginia Houses Along the James*. New York: Bonanza Books, 1957.

First Ladies Cookbook, The, by Margaret Brown Klapthor et al. Np: Parents' Magazine Press, 1965.

Furman, Bess, *White House Profile*. Indianapolis and New York: The Bobbs-Merrill Company, 1951.

Gouverneur, Marian, *As I Remember*. New York and London: D. Appleton & Co., 1911.

Hastings, Russell, *Genealogy and Autobiography of Russell Hastings*. (Unpublished.) Copy of manuscript in The Rutherford B. Hayes Library, Fremont, Ohio.

Holloway, Laura C., *The Ladies of the White House, or In the Home of the Presidents*. Philadelphia: Bradley & Company, 1881.

Hoover, Irwin Hood, *Forty-two Years in the White House*. Boston and New York: Houghton Mifflin Co., 1934.

Jensen, Amy LaFollette, *The White House and Its Thirty-four Families*. New York, Toronto and London: McGraw-Hill Book Company, 1958, 1962, 1965.

King, George H.S., "Bicentennial of the Birth of James Monroe," *Daughters of the American Revolution Magazine,* Vol. 92, No. 4, April, 1958.

Logan, Mrs. John A., editor, *Thirty Years in Washington, or Life and Scenes in Our National Capital*. Hartford, Conn: A. D. Worthington & Co., 1901.

Longworth, Alice Roosevelt, *Crowded Hours*. New York and London: Charles Scribner's Sons, 1933.

McAdoo, Eleanor Wilson, in collaboration with Margaret Y. Gaffey, *The Woodrow Wilsons*. New York: The Macmillan Co., 1937.

Morgan, George, *The Life of James Monroe*. Boston: Small, Maynard and Company, Publishers, 1921.

Porter, E. R., "Historic Weddings of the White House." *Pearson's Magazine,* Vol. 15, March, 1906.

Ross, Ishbel, *The General's Wife: The Life of Mrs. Ulysses S. Grant*. New York: Dodd Mead & Company, 1959.

Sadler, Christine, *America's First Ladies*. New York: Macfadden-Bartell Corp., 1963.

Sayre, Francis Bowes, *Glad Adventure*. New York: The MacMillan Co., 1957.

Seager, Robert II, *And Tyler, too*. New York, Toronto & London: McGraw-Hill Book Co., Inc., 1963.

Seaton, Josephine, *William Winston Seaton*. Boston: J. R. Osgood & Co., 1871.

Shelton, Isabelle, *The White House Today and Yesterday*. New York: Fawcett Publications Inc., 1962.

Singleton, Esther, *The Story of the White House*. London: Hodder & Stoughton, 1908. In two volumes, printed in United States of America.

Smith, Margaret Bayard, *The First Forty Years of Washington Society.* Edited by Gaillard Hunt. New York: Frederick Unger Publishing Co., republished 1965 from the first edition, published by Charles Scribner's Sons, 1906.

Stickley, Julia Ward, "Catholic Ceremonies in the White House, 1832-33; Andrew Jackson's Forgotten Ward, Mary Lewis." *Catholic Quarterly Review,* July 1965, pps. 192-198.

Sweetser, Kate Dickinson, *Famous Girls of the White House.* New York: Thomas Y. Crowell Company, 1930 and 1937.

Tayloe, Benjamin Ogle, *In Memoriam.* Compiled by Winslow M. Watson. Washington: 1872. Philadelphia: Sherman & Co., Printers.

Tyler, Lyon G., *Letters and Times of the Tylers,* Richmond, Virginia. 1884-1894.

Tyler Manuscript Material, Letters of Margaret Gardiner Beekman to Alexander Gardiner, John Tyler to Juliana McLachlin Gardiner, and Julia Gardiner Tyler to Juliana McLachlin Gardiner. New Haven, Conn.: Yale University Library.

Tyler Papers, Diary and letters of Priscilla Cooper Tyler. University, Ala.: University of Alabama Library.

Upton, Harriet Taylor, *Our Early Presidents.* Boston: D. Lothrop Company. 1890.

Wharton, Anne Hollingsworth, *Salons, Colonial and Republican.* Philadelphia and London: J. B. Lippincott and Co., 1900.

Wharton, Anne Hollingsworth, *Social Life in the Early Republic.* Philadelphia and London: J. B. Lippincott Company, 1903.

Wilcox, Pauline Burke, *Emily Donelson of Tennessee.* In two volumes. Richmond, Virginia: Garrett and Massie, Inc.

Willets, Gilson, *Inside Story of the White House.* New York: The Christian Herald, 1908.

Wilson, Edith Bolling, *My Memoir.* Indianapolis and New York: The Bobbs-Merrill Company, 1938-39.

Files of the following periodicals and newspapers contemporary with the weddings:

BOSTON POST
CHICAGO INTER-OCEAN
HARPER'S WEEKLY
LESLIE'S ILLUSTRATED WEEKLY
NATIONAL INTELLIGENCER
NEW YORK DAILY GRAPHIC
NEW YORK HERALD
NEW YORK WORLD
PHILADELPHIA PRESS
RICHMOND (VA.) ENQUIRER
THE WASHINGTON POST

Index